YES, LORD

Dom Edmund Jones is a Benedictine monk of the Congregation of Monte Oliveto. He was for many years parish priest of Christ the King, Cockfosters. He now belongs to the twin monasteries (of monks and nuns respectively) at Turvey in Bedfordshire.

He is Chairman of the Board of the ecumenical review *One in Christ*, and is well known for his broadcasts.

YES, LORD, I BELIEVE

by Dom Edmund M. Jones O.S.B.
monk of Turvey

Collins
FOUNT PAPERBACKS

First published by Fount Paperbacks, London, in 1985

© Edmund Jones 1985

Made and printed in Great Britain by
William Collins Sons & Co. Ltd, Glasgow

Cum approbatione auctoritatis ecclesiasticae

For M, who also believes

Jesus said [to Martha]:
"I am the resurrection and the life;
he who believes in me, though he die,
yet shall he live,
and whoever lives and believes in me
shall never die.
Do you believe this?"
She said to him,
"Yes, Lord;
I believe that you are the Christ,
the Son of God,
he who is coming into the world."
                    (John 11:25–27)

Contents

	Preface	9
1.	The Search	11
2.	The Many-Splendoured Thing	17
3.	The Breakthrough in Jesus of Nazareth	26
4.	The Ladder Betwixt Heaven and Charing Cross	33
5.	The Meaning of the Cross	41
6.	Seven Words from the Cross	50
7.	Life Through Death	56
8.	The Easter Victory	63
9.	The Spirit of Jesus	68
10.	About Prayer	72
11.	More About Prayer	77
12.	Creatures Great and Small	81
13.	Four "Moral" Travelogues	87
14.	Three Good Things in Life	94
15.	Three Words	100
16.	On Being Ordinary	106
17.	Society	110
18.	Thoughts at the Beginning of a New Year	117
19.	An Epilogue on Unity	121
	Acknowledgements	127

Preface

The chapters of this book are an edited form of broadcasts made on BBC television, Radio 4 and World Service. They have been left very much in "spoken form", but I have tried to group them in a connected narrative. The Epilogue was not broadcast but was given at Turvey as a talk during the Week of Prayer for Christian Unity 1984.

I would like to thank the BBC producers, particularly Father Pat McEnroe, who have helped me to tackle the microphone; and also a member of our sister community at Turvey who spent a lot of time tidying up the final text.

1. *The Search*

I wish I could see whom I am addressing – I don't mean whether you have brown hair or blue eyes or a long nose, but whether you are sad, or happy, or alone, or tired . . . I don't even know where you are. But the advantage is that had I in the ordinary way actually just met you we would hardly be likely to talk about anything except the weather, whereas this way we can, so to say, sit side by side, and, if you will allow me, I can think with you about other things.

I am a Benedictine monk. You may never have met one. What on earth is that all about? Let's say that I am a seeker, and I guess you may be one too: a seeker after the meaning of this life of ours. Oh, I know that a lot of the time we take it for granted – life is about having food to eat, a roof over one's head, about loving and being loved . . . but most of us, at least from time to time, want an answer that goes a bit deeper. I've come from where? I'm going to where? Is there a meaning to it all? Why am I here? We are all of us "seekers" after the truth. Not just whether it is true that the Red Sea exists, but the truth about life itself – what is it and where does it take us?

I remember when I was quite a small kid being bothered about this, and going outside one night and looking up into the sky wondering what space was, and where did the world end? Was there an end? What was there beyond the billion-billionth star? And I can distinctly remember my small tum turning over at the very thought, and then going back into the house . . .

That, I think, was my first conscious step in the search. Where had all that vast universe come from? Was it all that there was? Was there something beyond? Was there infinity, and what was infinity? If there was time, where did it end? It must end, but what was beyond time, what was eternity? Big questions for a little lad to answer.

Part of the answer I grew up with (because I was brought up in a Christian home) was that it all came from God. So who and what was God? He was our Father, I was told. My own father had died when I was only four, but I was very close to my two girl cousins and they had a super dad, my Uncle Arthur. So I suppose my ideas about this Father-God were largely based on him. And if somewhere behind this vast universe there was someone like my Uncle Arthur, then it was a good place to be in, for, although he could be quite strict and expected us kids to behave, we knew all the time that he loved us and we certainly loved him.

I'm not sure where "mother" fitted into all this. I think perhaps at this stage mother/father were not dissociated in my child's mind, and the God we talked about and talked to (and we did quite a bit of that) was father/mother rolled into one. Had my father/mother experience been an unhappy one I'm not sure how that would have affected my ideas about God and the world, but in fact I grew up with an image of God who was kind and loving and good for us. How much of that have I had to unlearn? Quite honestly, none of it. Now I've no idea, of course, how much of this experience is paralleled in yours – but I can tell you how for me the search proceeded.

The next stage came when I was at school. Until then though I had learned about Jesus ("Gentle Jesus, meek and mild, look upon this little child" was one of the prayers I was taught to say), I think the Father-God was more real to me. At school I came to a new understanding of who Jesus was – this God of the universe had "become man". This loving Father whom I had never seen, but who I firmly believed existed, had taken shape in a man called Jesus. It's true I had never seen him either, but I took for gospel truth what I was told about him, and all this tied up with that picture of God: this Jesus was good, and loving and kind, he had even died for me on the cross. I took to that idea like a duck to water. Yes, I liked Jesus!

The third stage was yet to come – to love Jesus. That came, I think, bit by bit. I know some people have a sudden illumination (a conversion experience like St Paul's), but I can't say that I ever did. For me it was just becoming gradually more and more real; I suppose, in a way, more real than my ideas about the Father-God. And certainly real enough for me to want to be a disciple: if I took him on board I would find the truth! And increasingly I came to believe that he *was* the Truth; that I wasn't in the end looking for truths, but for the Truth itself, for a person.

That is either immensely complex – what, after all, is more complex than a person, when or how can one fathom the depths of a person? – or quite incredibly simple, because the relationship would not be a complicated intellectual one of ideas and theories, but a relationship of persons, a relationship of love. So what started out as a stomach-turning wondering about infinity as a small boy became a love relationship. The next stage of the search was to be a lover, and that is a tantalizing process. One thing was pretty clear. If this was for real, there were no half measures, and sayings of Jesus in the gospels began to stand out of the page, sayings such as, "He who loves father or mother more than me is not worthy of me, cannot be my disciple" (cf. Matthew 10:37).

So in the end there seemed to be only one thing for me to do if I was serious in my search, if he was indeed the Truth. I had to hand myself over to him, commit myself to the Truth. And so I became a monk.

"Do you truly seek God?" is what a man is asked when he seeks to enter a monastery, with the promise that the way would not always be easy, the paths up the mountain of God are sometimes difficult and rugged. There was the ominous reminder that Jesus himself, on his way back to the Father, had to pass through brutal death and suffering. There was a necessary self-emptying if God was to enter; but he was there to be found. Somewhere within that framework I would find him. The question now is, did I find him?

The answer to that question is, I think, that I did and I didn't. I didn't in the sense that, after nearly forty years as a monk, I am still a long way from the final answer. I didn't in the sense that in the God-search there are periods of blackness, of blackness when he is hidden behind a cloud. I didn't in the sense that only the pure in heart see God, the really single-minded, and I have not arrived at such purity of heart.

But I *did* find him in the sense that I am more sure than ever that he is there. Never in my life have I been more convinced that HE IS, just as I am more than ever convinced that nothing can ever put me outside his love, that those everlasting arms of his are for real. I did find him in the sense that I have felt his presence so often in others; indeed, one of the reasons for joining a monastery is the fellowship of the brethren who help one in the search; and all sorts of other people I have met in the course of my priestly ministry have been windows onto God.

And this is, I believe, part of the common experience of the seeker; I hope that it is part of your own. The sky is not always a clear blue, clouds come and go; and part of the discovery itself is the very hiddenness of God, the infinite mystery of God who "dwells in unapproachable light" (1 Timothy 6:16). And we all of us suffer from that lack of purity of heart, with so many distractions which lead us away from our search. These things are our common experience. There is too the element of wrong-doing, of sin, of self-will, of self-seeking and self-concern; whereas to enter into the Absolute requires a self-emptying, as indeed it is said of Jesus himself that he "emptied himself, taking the form of a servant" and because he emptied himself he is now highly exalted and, as man, reigns within the Godhead (Philippians 2:7ff).

And, you know, even our failures are part of the path, part of the search, indeed an integral part of the search, because they highlight our total dependence on him. They are a vital discovery of our own nothingness until and unless we are taken up into God. So it is ever clearer to me that it is only in God and with God and through God that I can become, that I can indeed BE.

Nevertheless there is still an awareness that the mystery eludes me. What I have increasingly felt was the need for more space, for more stillness in the search. I don't mean particularly physical space or physical silence, though these things are certainly of great value. No, I mean a spiritual space around oneself, a still point in which one can be. Even in a monastery it is very easy to be filled up, for the whole day to be filled up with a sort of busy-ness, going from one thing to another (how much more so for people who live busy lives rushing hither and thither in cities!). One needs, as the poet says, time "to stand and stare" like sheep and cows, to let things simply drop away, to discover real stillness, real silence and simply to wait on God.

So I am now living in a new, very small, monastery where we are trying (not always very successfully) to make sure we have this "space" in our lives. It still means very much living with others – looking for God by being totally cut off from other people is a very special path, though there are those who tread it. But to be with other people who are engaged on the same search is great.

That is where I am at present. If the journey is up to the top of the mountain, I would say that I am still somewhere in the foothills; but the top of the mountain is there all right, beckoning me on (mountains do beckon!), and I travel confidently.

So, dear unknown friend, whoever or wherever you are,

who are climbing the same mountain into the Mystery by your own particular path (and there are many paths up the mountain), as you seek for the meaning of life, you and I are part of a large fellowship. This fellowship is not prepared to believe that life is without meaning, it is not able to believe that there is simply nothing beyond, that the anguish of this world of ours is quite without meaning and purposeless. If you are a Christian you will believe with me that the key to the mystery is Jesus Christ, that the suffering, loving Christ is the Mystery Revealed and that he is the Way as he is the Truth. At the end of the search there is not something but Someone, the end of the search is Love. And whoever you may be, we are being drawn into that search, all of us, by the One who is All, who is Love.

> *Does the road wind uphill all the way?*
>   *Yes, to the very end.*
> *Will the day's journey take the whole long day?*
>   *From morn to night, my friend.*
>
> *But is there for the night a resting place?*
>   *A roof for when the slow, dark hours begin?*
> *May not the darkness hide it from my face?*
>   *You cannot miss that inn.*
>
> *Shall I meet other wayfarers at night?*
>   *Those who have gone before.*
> *Then must I knock, or call when just in sight?*
>   *They will not keep you waiting at that door.*
>
> *Shall I find comfort, travel-sore and weak?*
>   *Of labour you shall find the sum.*
> *Will there be beds for me and all who seek?*
>   *Yes, beds for all who come.*
>   ("Up-Hill", by Christina Rossetti)

2. *The Many-Splendoured Thing*

You might be surprised (but then perhaps not) if I, a Benedictine monk, say that I had in my school locker two pin-ups. One was Carole Lombard (who was the Marilyn Monroe of the 1930s) and the other was Greta Garbo – Garbo, that superb tragic actress who had made the phrase "I want to be alone" as famous as Mae West's "Come up and see me sometime", but who never smiled. Oh, a goddess! And then she made a film in which she laughed. It was called *Ninotchka* and I went to see it four times, the last time when I had forty-eight hours' leave in Cairo during the war. In it Garbo played the part of a Russian commissar who had come to the West in a trade mission, terribly cold and clinical and "scientific". She fell first for Paris and then for a particular Parisian played by Adolphe Menjou, and there was a great love scene (done in the discreet way they used to do love scenes in the cinema). In it he looked into her eyes and said, "Your eyes are like stars", and she looked into his and said, "Your cornea is excellent".

Two ways of looking at things, and both of them saying something true. Of course, literally her eyes didn't look like stars. But doesn't the lover's vision say something more than (and more important than) the "scientific" fact?

The song I was crazy about at that time was a marvellous Cole Porter, "You're the Top": You're the Tower of Pisa, You're the smile on the Mona Lisa, You're Mickey Mouse, You're the Tops . . . I still love to hear it! And again the singer knows perfectly well that she doesn't really look like the Tower of Pisa any more than Solomon in the Song of Songs really thought the bridegroom had legs like stone pillars: "his eyes are like doves, his legs are alabaster columns set upon bases of gold" (5:12, 15). But the poetic vision is just so true! When "boy meets girl" you can describe the encounter in chemical terms – his hormones or chromosomes or whatever set up a chemical reaction in her – but when you have said that you haven't said half of what we mean by love. The love between two people isn't just physical, isn't just material – it has a spiritual dimension.

You could say the same sort of thing about friendship. You can look someone in the eyes and "see" there that you can trust him completely; but there isn't literally, physically, someone sitting there inside that little window.

You can analyse the human body in its various chemical components – I believe we prove to be very largely composed of water – but when you have said that you have by no means said MAN. You haven't said even the half of it when you have said the physically, clinically observable.

I'd guess that when they open their morning paper a good number of people, if they don't look first for page three or for the sports page, turn pretty quickly to the horoscopes. They are not my cup of tea at all, but I think their popularity (and the fact that they are even included in Breakfast TV) shows that a lot of people have at the back of their heads the idea that, as Shakespeare said, "there are more things in heaven and earth than are dreamt of in your philosophy". Because even if you say (as I would), for example, about superstitions,"I don't believe in all that nonsense", when I walk under a ladder quite boldly I still get that funny little feeling at the bottom of the spine which says, "Yes, but there just might be something in it."

Let's come back to the poetic vision. I once looked up the article on WIND in the *Encyclopaedia Britannica*, and this is the sort of thing I found:

The pattern of the general circulation is primarily

determined by the unequal heating of the
atmosphere at different latitudes and altitudes and
by the effect of the earth's rotation. Seasonal
variations of positions and intensity of these wind
belts are produced by the annual march of the sun,
and further complications are caused by the
physical differences between water and land . . .

And it is, of course, all perfectly true. But if you look
outside and see the wind blowing the autumn leaves here,
there and everywhere, would you not, like me, find
Shelley's picture of wind just as telling?

> *O wild West Wind, thou breath of Autumn's being,*
> *Thou, from whose unseen presence the leaves dead*
> *Are driven, like ghosts from an enchanter fleeing.*
>
> *Yellow, and black, and pale, and hectic red,*
> *Pestilence-stricken multitudes . . .*

Isn't that a fantastically *true* picture of the leaves being
whirled here and there by the wind, and don't we, when we
hear it, recognize the poet's vision as *real*?

Then there is the poem we all had to learn –
Wordsworth's "Daffodils":

> *I wandered lonely as a cloud*
> *That floats on high o'er vales and hills,*
> *When all at once I saw a crowd,*
> *A host, of golden daffodils . . .*

We used to rattle it off in a great sing-song gabble, but if
you go back to it now and read it carefully you will find that
the poet has really expressed something true and
important. What is happening is that the poet gets behind
the surface of things and finds a unity, a wholeness, a

significance which clicks and which we know instinctively to be true.

Go into the National Gallery, for instance, and see a splendid painting like Turner's "Fighting Temeraire"; if you look at the detail of the paint, well, of course, it isn't the literal colour of sea or ships or sky at all, and yet the total vision of the artist makes you say, "But it is *exactly* like that."

I've mentioned poetry and art so I might as well mention music too. Is a piece of music really nothing more than a series of verifiable sound waves and frequencies? Or is there some spark, some flame of genius that makes you curl up with sheer joy as you listen to a Vivaldi Concerto? Some of us are musically tone deaf, and a whole range of experience is then cut off. Some people don't "see" when they go into a picture gallery; but that doesn't alter the fact of the artist's vision. When somebody who had got bored in the National Gallery said to one of the attendants that he didn't think much of the pictures, he was told, "It is not the pictures which are being judged, it is you", because it is possible to be blocked to a whole range of experiences, to be love-deaf, to be colour-blind. It is possible to miss the "vision". Francis Thompson, who was a Thames drop-out two generations ago, says it beautifully:

> *O World invisible, we view thee,*
> *O World intangible, we touch thee,*
> *O World unknowable, we know thee,*
> *Inapprehensible, we clutch thee! . . .*
>
> *The angels keep their ancient places—*
> *Turn but a stone and start a wing!*
> *'Tis ye, 'tis your estrangèd faces*
> *That miss the many-splendoured thing.*
> ("The Kingdom of God")

The Many-Splendoured Thing

The many-splendoured thing – that is a reality. Take something more controversial, for instance, something like Uri Geller and his spoon-bending. Some people, I know, think it is just a great conjuring trick, but I quote him simply as an example of the sort of area of which from time to time we have to take notice. There is a whole world of paranormal phenomena, for which there is plenty of well-established, clinically observed evidence. You may recall some of the strange things in Lyall Watson's *Supernature* (geraniums that grow faster if you play them a Bach Brandenburg Concerto, and so on). A whole dimension lies there where we cross the border between the purely physical and what, for want of a better word, I am going to call a spiritual dimension. There is a whole range of human experience which cannot be card indexed and tabulated. All through the centuries, and in every conceivable country and civilization, there have been countless men and women who have spoken of the way they have experienced this "mystic" reality. And when I say every conceivable civilization I mean it; people of all religions and none have spoken and written of an experience they found totally overwhelming, experience of a reality beneath or behind or beyond (words begin to be totally inadequate here), of a oneness of being, of a something which was rich and marvellous and satisfying and beckoning and . . . and everything.

In India centuries ago one such mystic had this to say of his experience:

> Shining, yet hidden, Spirit lives in the
> cavern. Everything that sways, breathes, opens,
>   closes,
> lives in Spirit; beyond learning, beyond everything,
> better than anything; living, unliving.
> It is the undying, blazing Spirit, that seed
> of all seeds wherein lay hidden the

> *world and all its creatures. It is life,*
> *speech, mind, reality, immortality . . .*
>   (from the Mundaka-Upanishad)

That was a Hindu. This is an experience of a nine year old girl as she told it later in life:

> **Suddenly the Thing happened, and, as everybody knows, it cannot be described in words. The Bible phrase, "I saw the heavens open", seems as good as any if not taken literally. I remember saying to myself, in awe and rapture, "So it's like this; now I know what Heaven is like, now I know what they mean in Church." The words of the Twenty-third Psalm came into my head and I began repeating them: "He maketh me to lie down in green pastures; He leadeth me beside the still waters." Soon it faded and I was alone in the meadow with the baby and the brook and the sweet-smelling lime trees. But though it passed and only the earthly beauty remained, I was filled with great gladness, I had seen the "far distances".**
>
> (Quoted from Margaret Isherwood, *The Root of the Matter* [Gollancz] in F. C. Happold's *Mysticism* [Pelican Books]. The Indian quotation above, and the Sufi quotation which follows are from the same book.)

The Muslims have come to the same reality:

> *As salt resolved in ocean*
> *I was swallowed in God's sea,*
> *Past faith, past unbelieving,*
> *Past doubt, past certainty.*
>
> *Suddenly in my bosom*
> *A star shone clear and bright;*

All the suns of heaven
Vanished in that star's light.

> (Rumi, a Sufi mystic and poet)

And in contemporary Christian experience there is the same awareness of SPIRIT around us in so many ways:

Spirit of God in the clear running water,
blowing to greatness the trees on the hill.
Spirit of God in the finger of morning,
fill the earth, bring it to birth
and blow where you will.
Blow, blow, blow till I be
but breath of the Spirit blowing in me.

> (Sister Miriam-Therese Winter)

I don't want to push my point too hard – if there is loveliness behind so much of our experience (beauty, love, courage, unselfishness . . .) there is also sometimes a chilling forbiddingness. To climb Everest must be an exhilarating and hauntingly beautiful experience for the mountaineer, but it is also a tragic place which can bring an expedition icily to an end.

Philosophers have tried again and again over the centuries to ferret out the meaning of it all – from the "Fate" of the Greeks (one of the great theatre experiences of my life was Laurence Olivier's horrendous cry in *Oedipus Rex* as he stumbled, blinded, down the steps of his palace, the victim of Fate) to Sartre's view of life as the "Theatre of the Absurd".

So is there something there? I want to say YES. But is it something cold and clammy like some science fiction horror from outer space? As a Christian I believe that the spirit thing, the spirit dimension, that which lies behind and beneath and within everything that exists (whatever way you choose to say it), revealed itself in Jesus of

Nazareth. The glimpses we get of the "many-splendoured thing" are little breakthroughs from that dimension, but there was a super-breakthrough in Jesus. Jesus of Nazareth was completely the expression of that Spirit, a perfect and unique expression, and in him we know what it is. In him we know what that Spirit behind everything is.

But I begin with what I take as a fact: that if, as Francis Thompson says, we turn but a stone, we start a wing. That there is more in heaven and earth. That to say to your wife "Your eyes are like stars", surprised though she may be if you haven't said it for ages, is to say something true. That there is a whole world, a whole dimension waiting to be revealed. That there are far distances which can be glimpsed if we have eyes that see – because that same Jesus of Nazareth has warned us that there are those who see and yet see nothing, who hear and yet hear nothing.

There is a song, though I can't say that I've heard it lately, which is appropriate at this point:

> *I don't know your name and I won't call you God*
> *for that name has grown slipshod*
> *and easy to say,*
> *but I'll talk to you, talk to you*
> *all my life long,*
> *and perhaps you will answer me, answer some day.*
>
> *I wait in the silence*
> *and all that I hear*
> *is the pulse of my heart beating*
> *lively and strong;*
> *yet the gift of the promise that beats through my*
> *   blood*
> *makes me hope for you, search for you,*
> *all my life long.*

The Many-Splendoured Thing

They say that you're there
in the flower and the star,
that the wind through my hair
brings a message from you;
but my heart needs a human
response to its cry,
a face in its mirror
that seems human too.

Sometimes from the shadows
you seem to step forth
in the people I meet who are
friendly and kind,
in a moment of loving,
a gesture of warmth;
yet these can't make easy
the ache in my mind.

I don't know your name and I won't call you God,
for that name has grown slipshod
and easy to say;
but I'll talk to you, talk to you
all my life long,
and perhaps you will answer me, answer some day.

3. The Breakthrough in Jesus of Nazareth

From all sides, if we have eyes to see, if we have ears to hear, we can become aware of a "presence", of a spirit dimension to life, which goes way beyond the purely physical. It is the message of a favourite old hymn:

O Lord my God, when I in awesome wonder
Consider all the worlds thy hand has made,
I see the stars, I hear the rolling thunder,
Thy pow'r throughout the universe displayed,
Then sings my soul, my Saviour God, to thee:
How great thou art, how great thou art!

When through the woods and forest glades I wander
And hear the birds sing sweetly in the trees,
When I look down from lofty mountain grandeur,
And hear the brook and feel the gentle breeze,
Then sings my soul, my Saviour God, to thee:
How great thou art, how great thou art!

And that is all around us – take the artistry of the football field which lifts a game up beyond the mere physical displacement of a ball from point A to B to C to goal. It is more than purely physical, there is a magic about it.

And, too, there is always that unexplained longing and searching and unsatisfied desire . . . Augustine of Hippo, who had experimented with most things in order to satisfy this longing, finally found the answer (for himself at least) and wrote his *Confessions*, one of the world's greatest explorations of man's personality, in which he said: "God, you have made us for yourself, and our hearts are restless till they find their rest in you . . . Beauty, old and ever new, too late have I loved you." Augustine had found his answer.

From the same continent, Africa, but much further south, from Bantu country, comes this:

> *We are outside*
> *because of our weariness,*
> *because of our tears.*
> *Oh, for a place in heaven!*
>
> *Oh, if I had wings to fly there!*
> *If a strong rope came down*
> *I would seize it and climb it*
> *and I would go up*
> *and live there.*

If only we could make real contact! Side by side with the witnesses to the fact that there is something there, is the longing of the human spirit to be "in touch with it", to "discover it", to "uncover it", to "know". Ancient Israel knew the same longing: "Shower, O heavens, from above, and let the skies rain down righteousness . . . Comfort, comfort my people, says your God" (Isaiah 45:8; 40:1). They longed for and they received a promise of the great revelation to come: "And the glory of the Lord shall be revealed, and all flesh shall see it together, for the mouth of the Lord has spoken" (Isaiah 40:5).

In the first chapter I recalled going out into the garden on a clear starry night, when I was only a boy, looking up into the sky and wondering what was there, where the borders of space ended, what lay beyond, and was there in fact a beyond? Now that I know more about what the scientists say of the size and shape of the universe I find it all the more fascinating, and more than ever I wonder what is "out there". I find it impossible to imagine that there is no life "out there", that in all the billions and billions of worlds ours alone should be inhabited, should have life. I am also quite certain that if our scientists should discover the existence of intelligent beings somewhere "out there" they would go crazy to get in touch. And that is what the spirit does – it moves out, it probes, it searches.

And it seems to me quite obvious that if the spirit dimension exists, if there *is* a spirit thing, it will seek to break through to us and our consciousness, just as you can bet your bottom dollar our scientists would want to break through to other beings in space. Now I may block this breakthrough in all sorts of ways by being "deaf", "blind", "turned in on myself", "otherwise engaged", and my awareness of spirit may be limited, but the Spirit does still try to break through. As a Christian I believe that the great breakthrough came in Jesus of Nazareth, that this was a man so filled with the Spirit, so "open" to the Spirit, that in human terms he was a perfect expression, a unique expression of the Spirit. And Christians struggling to understand this have therefore talked about him as divine – Lord and God – Son of God – God-Man.

What we see in Jesus is not some wishy-washy, milk-and-water, stained-glass window figure. Anthony Burgess, talking about him in a TV programme, once said:

> I see him more or less as T. S. Eliot described him in one of his poems, "Christ the Tiger", not gentle Jesus, meek and mild. But a tigerish temper, tigerish intelligence, exhorting people to love their enemies, but being most vehement about it.

This is Spirit present in power and force. And what we see and hear is LOVE.

> That which was from the beginning, which we have heard, which we have seen with our eyes, which we

have looked upon and touched with our hands, concerning the word of life – the life was made manifest, and we saw it, and testify to it, and proclaim to you the eternal life which was with the Father and was made manifest to us – that which we have seen and heard we proclaim also to you, so that you may have fellowship with us; and our fellowship is with the Father and with his Son Jesus Christ. And we are writing this that our joy may be complete . . . Beloved, let us love one another; for love is of God, and he who loves is born of God and knows God. He who does not love does not know God; for God is love . . . God is love, and he who abides in love abides in God, and God abides in him (1 John 1:1–3; 4:7–8, 16).

In the end it was out of love that he died. And in dying, so the New Testament claims, he was expressing to us and for us the love of that Spirit which is behind all that exists. "God so loved the world that he gave his only Son . . . Father, forgive them; for they know not what they do" (John 3:16; Luke 23:34). The Spirit behind all that exists, and whom we see in Jesus, is Love. Not a spirit of hate, not a spirit of cruelty, not a spirit of destruction, not a spirit of death, not nasty and beastly and malignant, but a spirit of love. And that is the great revelation.

It not only revealed to us what is behind everything, it also showed us what happens to love, which is that it comes into conflict with the ugly power of evil and defeats it. It was a love which so totally accepted, so totally identified itself with every limitation of human flesh, even death, that it became totally free. Total acceptance meant total liberation.

> *They crucified my Lord*
> *and he never said a mumbalin' word,*

> *they crucified my Lord*
> *and he never said a mumbalin' word,*
> *not a word, not a word, not a word.*

He, the great Spirit of Love, accepted in love the total human condition, and in love the Spirit brought Jesus through death to life and resurrection. He was and he is the Way. The whole wonderful universe reaches its climax in Jesus, the Risen Jesus.

All the limitations of time and space and everything fell away, they went, they were dissolved, the whole lot; and he, the Risen Jesus, became totally, sovereignly open, liberated, universal, perfect man!

That is spirit-power. You may well have seen it in someone suffering and conquering, but we see it supremely in Jesus. It set him wonderfully free and alive.

> *Humbled for a season,*
> *to receive a name*
> *from the lips of sinners*
> *unto whom he came,*
> *faithfully he bore it*
> *spotless to the last,*
> *brought it back victorious*
> *when from death he passed.*

I once witnessed baptism by immersion in a Baptist church (I'm glad to say that the new Roman Catholic rite of Baptism envisages this happening amongst us) and what I saw was a young woman being "drowned" – dying symbolically in the water, and in the name of Jesus rising to her new life with him. Well, that is what happened, not symbolically but in reality to Jesus: by going down into the depths, into death and all that it implied, he rose again to a new existence. For him personally this was the fulfilment of all that he was – this was his "perfection". But it is a perfection which he wishes to share with us.

So let us say that there is a spirit dimension to life; let us say that it breaks through to us in Jesus of Nazareth; and let us say that in Jesus of Nazareth it really fulfilled itself: where does it take us?

Ages ago one of the colour supplements had a front page cover which tried to show just how old the world is, how old life is and how old man is, by comparing them to the time scale of twenty-four hours. Not all that long ago people used to think that the world began in 4004 B.C., some six thousand years ago. Now we know that it is billions of years old, that it existed long, long before life first appeared and that anything recognizably human appeared a very long time after that. So this front page had rows and rows of clocks, starting with one showing midnight and so on up to the next midnight, and the whole of those twenty-four hours represented the age of the world. And on that scale, as I remember it, life began to appear not in the earth's early morning but at about five minutes to midnight; and man at only a few seconds before midnight. Now if that is the time scale, the evolutionary process is surely only just getting off the ground, and it is unthinkable that you and I are the end products – we are primitive creatures still. In a billion years' time they could look back on us and say, "How ape-like!" After all, look at the idea that in order to communicate with someone else I have to keep making funny noises – there is clearly an immense potential for development.

But then suppose that in Jesus of Nazareth the whole process took a great leap forward, that the Risen Jesus leapt out of the time sequence into the future – that the totally living, totally loving, totally liberated, totally universal Jesus is the perfect man, "super-man" if you like, the *end* product. That is what pre-history and history are all about, and he is calling us into that new world, into that new creation of which he is the "number one man", the new Adam.

I believe that Jesus, the great breakthrough from the Spirit, alive now more than ever, is calling you and me, beckoning you and me forward, to step into the unknown with him, to walk on the water!

Spirit God, I've known you in all sorts of ways. You have touched me in all sorts of ways. I have known you above all in Jesus, and I believe that through him I can come into oneness with all that is, that I can find wholeness, can find freedom, can find you. Show me more, Lord!

4. The Ladder Betwixt Heaven and Charing Cross

If you have given or received love, that is a glimpse of that other dimension, the "many-splendoured thing", which is constantly breaking through the surface of things. Sometimes we see that love as romantic – "Some enchanted evening" – but it can also be very unromantic (and even more real) when it is, for instance, the patient and wearisome visiting of a long-term hospital patient. But wherever there is love it is the spirit breaking through, the spirit which made its supreme breakthrough into our world in the person of Jesus of Nazareth, and which carried him through death, through time and space and out onto the other side, timeless and free.

And the spirit, his Spirit, is calling you and me into his new world, into a new kind of world, into what he calls "the kingdom", the kingdom of God, the upside-down world characterized in an unexpected insight many years ago by H. G. Wells in his *Outline of World History*:

> In the white blaze of this kingdom of his there was to be no property, no privilege, no pride and precedence; no motive indeed and no reward but love. Is it any wonder that men were dazzled and blinded and cried out against him? Even his disciples cried out when he would not spare them the light . . . For to take him seriously was to enter upon a strange and alarming life, to abandon habits, to control instincts and impulses, to essay an incredible happiness.

That spirit which breaks through from behind the surface

of things is the spirit of Love – that is the great revelation. Where LOVE is there GOD is.

And Jesus, the great breakthrough of the Spirit, promised that that spirit, his Spirit, would be given to all who asked it. To that first group of friends of Jesus, that first group who had been attracted by the sheer goodness of the man, the Godliness of the man, he promised that the Spirit would be poured out on them. "Wait for the promise of the Father, which, he said, 'you heard from me, for John baptized with water, but before many days you shall be baptized with the Holy Spirit'" (Acts 1:4–5). And on the Jewish Feast of Pentecost, fifty days after Jesus had experienced in his own person the spirit-power which had released him from death, the promise was fulfilled:

> **When the day of Pentecost had come, they were all together in one place. And suddenly a sound came from heaven like the rush of a mighty wind, and it filled all the house where they were sitting. And there appeared to them tongues as of fire, distributed and resting on each one of them. And they were all *filled with the Holy Spirit* (Acts 2:1–4).**

That Spirit came upon them in power, as it had on Jesus, and it took them through fire and water, driving and impelling them to tell everywhere about the great revelation.

One member of the original group, the one closest to Jesus, was the young John. He lived on to a very great age, long after the others were dead, and according to St Jerome, who had obviously picked up the story somewhere in the Middle East where he had gone to live, the old apostle John only had one thing to say to his followers day after day: "Little children, love one another." Now even the best of sermons (and the shortest) begins to pall if you have to listen to it every day, and so, according to St Jerome (who was, incidentally, a very serious and devoted Bible scholar), they went to St John one day with a kind of protest demo and asked why he never said anything else. And the old man, this close friend and intimate of Jesus, who had spent a long life in the service of the Master and in meditation on the Gospel, said, "Little children, love one another; for when you have done that you have done everything." That was someone who lived and breathed the Spirit of Jesus. No wonder then that those who, century by century, have been fascinated by Jesus of Nazareth have asked for that gift of his Spirit. "Spirit of the living God, fall afresh on me; melt me, mould me, fill me, use me. Spirit of the living God, fall afresh on me!" And always that Spirit is active. How indeed could you stop it? For it is the great Spirit of the universe, the great Creator Spirit which stirs the depths of the whole of creation, that something which is afoot in the universe, the omnipresent Spirit. It is the Spirit at work in all creative efforts – the artist, the builder, the engineer, the chemist – how can it be still? And it is above all present in men and women as they come to fullness in their year by year, day by day, re-creation of the Jesus pattern in their lives.

> *Enable with perpetual light*
> *The dullness of our blinded sight:*
>
> *Anoint and cheer our soilèd face*
> *With the abundance of thy grace . . .*
>
> *Teach us to know the Father, Son,*
> *And thee, of Both, to be but one.*

He is the "celestial fire", the fire of the universe, he is the "perpetual light", the "abundance of grace"; and the gift of the Spirit means nothing less than a sharing in the life

35

of the Godhead. The indwelling presence of the Spirit of the Living God, the union person-to-person of us with God, that taking on and being taken into the pattern of Jesus, that Christianization, is all a process of divinization. As the second letter of St Peter has it, "through the knowledge of him who called us to his own glory and excellence, by which he has granted to us his precious and very great promises, that through these you may escape from the corruption that is in the world because of passion, and become partakers of the divine nature" (2 Peter 1:3–4).

How can we identify this divine life? Well, take an obvious, easy example: Francis of Assisi. He is the man who, I think, more than most would spring to people's minds if one were looking for someone really (almost literally) Christ-like. He was the son of wealthy parents, merchants, in a bustling mediaeval city, handsome, gifted, charming, the leader of the town's blades and *the* big catch for any girl in Assisi. When he found Christ his whole life-style changed: there was a total indifference to material possessions and he lived a life of extreme simplicity, but joined to a lovely appreciation of all good things, of the whole creation. He had a totally non-materialistic possessiveness joined to an immense delight in things, and a desire to embrace everybody and everything in love. There was a total acceptance of the human condition, including suffering and what he called his Sister, Death. There was a total lovingness towards others, and his whole life-style was summed up in the prayer:

> *Lord, make me an instrument of your peace.*
> *Where there is hatred, let me sow love.*
> *Where there is friction, let me sow union.*
> *Where there is error, let me sow truth.*
> *Where there is doubt, let me sow faith.*
> *Where there is despair, let me sow hope.*

> *Where there is darkness, let me sow light.*
> *Where there is sadness, let me sow joy.*
> *Grant that I may not so much seek*
> *to be consoled as to console,*
> *to be understood as to understand,*
> *to be loved as to love.*
> *For it is in giving that we receive.*
> *It is in pardoning that we are pardoned.*
> *It is in dying that we rise again to eternal life.*

Does that not breathe the very spirit of Jesus? Francis was truly a Spirit-indwelt man. But he lived seven hundred years ago. How about someone nearer to today? I once visited Turin and went there especially to go to a place where the doorway is inscribed "The Little House of Divine Providence", and when it was built it really was the door into a little house. Today it serves as a doorway into what is in effect a city of some ten thousand people. The "little house" was started in the last century by a certain Joseph Cottolengo, as a refuge for people for whom society could or would do nothing. Today it is a *city* of refuge – for orphans, for cripples, for the sick and dying, for mental patients, etc., etc. It is run on the principle on which it has been based from the beginning, the Gospel principle of Jesus, that if we do God's will, if above all else we seek the kingdom of God and his righteousness, we can leave the rest to him, he will provide.

I was there on a Saturday afternoon, and I remember that in front of the altar in the chapel there was an empty flower vase – they were quite certain that God would send the flowers for Sunday. It is something when an individual has that kind of faith, but when a whole institution operates on that basis it is an eye-opener.

But the reason I want to tell you about it is that there is within the grounds a large mental hospital. You know those programmes where they say to the panel, "What was your most embarrassing moment?'' and the stars or personalities try to relate something unexpected or amusing which will entertain. Well, I will tell you what for me was truly the most embarrassing moment in the whole of my life, except that the word for it is not so much embarrassing as humiliating. I was taken into this mental hospital by a sister and almost immediately some poor man ran up to us and I felt embarrassed, but then we went into a large room which was a babble of meaningless noises and abnormal ''cases''. One man came up and made weird noises at me, and I began to sweat and wanted to get out. But that was not to be. The sister walked me slowly round the room, I getting more and more hot under the collar. She stopped from time to time to cuddle one of ''them'' and I was just dying to get out of the place. Afterwards when she was asked, ''What do they understand?'', the answer she gave was, ''They understand one thing: that we love them.'' I just wanted to get away – and she ''loved'' them! I can still remember how humiliated I felt. She was someone who had been touched by the Spirit of Jesus. Such folk don't have St written in front of their names (and if they did you might think them out of our league altogether) but you can, I'm sure, think of someone perfectly ordinary who is in fact quite extraordinary because touched by that same Spirit, the manifold Spirit. It is said of Evelyn Waugh that when he was reproached for behaving abominably he replied, ''Think how much worse I would have been had I not been a Catholic''. The grace of the Spirit works in all sorts of ways; but we can identify the Jesus pattern best and most easily when we see love in action.

> *I sought for God, but him I could not see;*
> *I sought for my soul, but it eluded me;*
> *I sought for my brother and I found all three.*

The Ladder Betwixt Heaven and Charing Cross

There's nothing automatic about it – it may indeed be a long slow struggle. It is a process of opening one's heart to receive, and to defeat in ourselves that element which is constantly at war with the Spirit. The "world", as St John calls it (by which he means life organized without reference to God), is continually at war with the Spirit, and little by little the world can be conquered in the power of that Spirit which conquered even death in Jesus of Nazareth.

The world is where we are, not just me in my personal situation (though it is that too) but the whole society, the whole political structure, where those filled with the Spirit must take their place in the warfare. What nonsense to think that religion has nothing to do with politics! We have to build the upside-down world of the Kingdom of God, the City of God. We have to pull this world into the "new world" where "Man" will be "Man-perfected" in the "image of Christ" who is the "image of God". It is here below that we must build. Archbishop William Temple once said that Christianity is the most materialistic of the world religions, falsely made into an otherworldly cult. Jacob's ladder is now, as Francis Thompson wrote, betwixt heaven and Charing Cross.

> *The angels keep their ancient places –*
> *Turn but a stone and start a wing!*
> *'Tis ye, 'tis your estrangèd faces*
> *That miss the many-splendoured thing.*
>
> *But (when so sad thou canst not sadder)*
> *Cry – and upon thy so sore loss*
> *Shall shine the traffic of Jacob's ladder*
> *Pitched betwixt Heaven and Charing Cross.*
>
> *Yea, in the night, my Soul, my daughter,*
> *Cry – clinging Heaven by the hems;*
> *And lo, Christ walking on the water*
> *Not of Gennesareth, but Thames!*

Yes, Lord, I Believe

Yes, it is not in some "Holy" Land far, far away that we shall find Christ. It is here that the City of God must be built. It is here that we must allow the Spirit to break through, it is our society that we must lend our hands to transform.

5.   *The Meaning of the Cross*

I begin with that cry *Eloi, Eloi, lama sabachthani* recorded for us in St Mark's Gospel, uttered by the carpenter's son from Nazareth, that cry of desolation, "My God, my God, why have you forsaken me?" Why is it that after all these years and all over the world people remember the death of a nobody, a small-town preacher? Why should it demand such attention? And why in the face of such agony and dereliction, such pointless brutality, why should the day of his death be called "Good" Friday? What is it about the scene? – after all, it is by no means the only crucifixion that history records. Josephus, the first-century Jewish historian, tells of one revolt against the Romans which ended with the mass crucifixion of two thousand rebels, and many men and women have died deaths just as ugly and as painful. What is it about that scene that has made artists throughout the world and throughout the centuries paint it, carve it, bejewel it, sing it, worship it?

It is that behind that horror there was something victorious, there was a power of love which transformed and conquered. However much, however realistically the artist has painted the vileness of the scene, that has never been it all. Every moment of those hours on the cross was a moment of battle, cosmic battle. "Death and Life met in a strange conflict" we sing on Easter Day, and Life won.

The mystery of Good Friday and Easter is one mystery. In the darkness there is light. There really is a silver lining to the cloud. There is a twofold truth: he went down into the depths and there found a glory which can never be taken from him. So there are two poles: the horror and the tragedy; the triumph and the glory. The human and the divine brought low; the human and the divine raised up.

The first sight is of the denuded Christ. I recall, when I was a novice in our monastery in Italy, praying before a hauntingly beautiful crucifix, carved in wood, where the life seemed to drain from the body of the dying man. It was the only one of his possessions that the rich Sienese lawyer, who founded the monastery in the fourteenth century, had kept when he left everything to seek for God in prayer and solitude, identifying himself with the total stripping of the crucified Christ. I recall too the singing on Good Friday of the Lamentations of Jeremiah as tragedy fell on the people of God and on the Son of God. But on that other note I remember seeing in Ravenna, that city of mosaic marvels, in the ancient chapel of the Archbishops, a mosaic of Christ dressed as a young Roman army officer with his pips up, complete with cross, his feet firmly planted on the defeated devil, triumphant in victory.

I recall, on the other hand, those disturbing, glowing paintings of Rouault, where the image of Christ, crowned with thorns, merges into the image of a circus clown, a tragico-pathetic figure which hints at yet another aspect of the cross, an aspect which I found most moving in *Godspell* with David Essex singing out his last breath, "Oh God, I'm dying, Oh God, I'm dead."

I recall that splendid Anglo-Saxon poem, "The Dream of the Rood", a vision in which the tree that bore our Saviour speaks of Christ coming to his cross:

> *The King of all mankind coming in great haste,*
> *With courage keen, eager to climb me.*
> *I did not dare, against my Lord's dictate,*
> *To bow down or break, though I beheld tremble*
> *The earth's four corners. I could easily*
> *Have felled his foes; yet fixed and firm I stood.*
> *Then the young Hero – it was God Almighty –*
> *Strong and steadfast, stripped himself for battle;*

The Meaning of the Cross

He climbed up on the high gallows, constant in his
purpose,
Mounted it in sight of many, mankind to ransom.
Horror seized me when the Hero clasped me.
But I dared not bow or bend down to earth,
Nor falter, nor fall; firm I needs must stand.
I was raised up a Rood, a royal King I bore,
The High King of heaven: hold firm I must.

You will recall that splendid Latin hymn *Vexilla Regis* which J. M. Neale translated splendidly as "The royal banners forward go". The ancient plainchant is said to have been originally a marching tune of the Roman legionaries as they quick-stepped to the conquest of the world. How that conjures up an image of the cross! It reminds me of Laurence Olivier's film of *Henry V* – that great dressed army, banners flowing, surging forward. Love and Life go forward. Love went forward to victory!

Mind you, you sometimes start understanding things when the atmosphere isn't at all religious. I remember being on pilgrimage in Jerusalem, and going with a group of friends along the traditional Way of the Cross. That wasn't at all religious. It was totally unlike any church service. There were no reverent bystanders. There was the souk, the covered street market, narrow and crowded with shops on either side and all the excited chatter of a Jerusalem going about its business – water-carriers, donkeys pushing past, Arab boys laden with boxes, shoving and darting, and through all this we struggled and straggled running to catch up with the others. One lady had to suffer the indignity of having her bottom pinched as we came to Calvary itself. And I think I realized for the first time just how very "unreligious" was the way to the cross that Jesus walked – past a mêlée of people, either hostile or indifferent, much more concerned about buying and selling.

I think of those stones in Jerusalem, uncovered only in the 1930s, having been hidden since the Roman period, part of the pavement of the Antonia Fortress which many believe to have been the residence of the Roman Procurator Pilate, come up to Jerusalem from his sea coast palace at Caesarea for Passover in case of trouble. And there Jesus was condemned to death by that governor, and there scratched in the floor is the Roman soldiers' version of Crown and Anchor, with which they amused themselves as they waited for their prisoners.

I recall too another scratched drawing in the plaster of one of the houses of the Imperial Palace on the Palatine Hill in Rome, a graffito scratched by some nasty page boy in the first century – a crucified donkey with, at the side, a kneeling figure and the words "Alaxamenos worships his god!" How many images! We have an eye witness account of it all from John, the disciple especially loved by Jesus, of whose account it is written, "This is the disciple who is bearing witness to these things, and who has written these things; and we know that his testimony is true" (21:24).

> When the soldiers had crucified Jesus they took his garments and made four parts, one for each soldier; also his tunic. But the tunic was without seam, woven from top to bottom; so they said to one another, "Let us not tear it, but cast lots for it to see whose it shall be." This was to fulfil the scripture, "They parted my garments among them, and for my clothing they cast lots."
>
> So the soldiers did this. But standing by the cross of Jesus were his mother, and his mother's sister, Mary the wife of Clopas, and Mary Magdalene. When Jesus saw his mother, and the disciple whom he loved standing near, he said to this mother, "Woman, behold your son!" Then he said to the

disciple, "Behold your mother!" And from that hour the disciple took her to his own home.

After this Jesus, knowing that all was now finished, said (to fulfil the scripture), "I thirst." A bowl full of vinegar stood there; so they put a sponge full of the vinegar on hyssop and held it to his mouth. When Jesus had received the vinegar, he said, "It is finished"; and he bowed his head and gave up his spirit.

Since it was the day of Preparation, in order to prevent the bodies from remaining on the cross on the sabbath (for that sabbath was a high day), the Jews asked Pilate that their legs might be broken, and that they might be taken away. So the soldiers came and broke the legs of the first, and of the other who had been crucified with him; but when they came to Jesus and saw that he was already dead, they did not break his legs. But one of the soldiers pierced his side with a spear, and at once there came out blood and water. He who saw it has borne witness – his testimony is true and he knows that he tells the truth – that you also may believe (John 19:23–35).

And it is precisely John, who saw this take place, who gives us the clue to the other side. "NOW is the Son of Man glorified. When I am lifted up from the earth I will draw all men to myself." He wasn't being dragged to the cross, he went willingly. He went willingly to a brutal, unjust death. The people from whom he might have expected support deserted him; the executioners were not at all anxious to spare him any of the indignity or suffering; and he hangs, nailed to the cross.

As he hung there he prayed, and from his lips came Psalm 21, a psalm of his ancestor David which he had known from his youth, familiar to those standing there:

"My God, my God, why have you forsaken me? . . . You are far from my plea and the cry of my distress . . . Oh my God, I call by day and you give no reply; I call by night and I find no peace."

"My God, my God, why have you forsaken me?" – the cry of a lonely man, of an anguished man, of a frightened man, a man dying and needing to know that God is near and knowing desolation, the man Jesus of Nazareth who had left his village to preach a message from the God who was now silent, the God he had trusted, the God who had always delivered his people in past ages. "You, O God, are holy, enthroned on the praises of Israel. In you our fathers put their trust; they trusted and you set them free. When they cried out to you, they escaped. In you they trusted and never in vain." My God, my God, why have you forsaken ME?

To what an extremity he has been reduced: "I am a worm and no man, the butt of men, laughing-stock of the people. All who see me deride me. They curl their lips, they toss their heads. 'He trusted in the Lord, let him save him; let him release him if this is his friend.'" As Jesus recited the psalm his enemies took it up with him to taunt him: "So also the chief priests, with the scribes and elders, mocked him, saying, 'He saved others; he cannot save himself . . . he trusts in God; let God deliver him now, if he desires him; for he said, I am the Son of God.' And the robbers who were crucified with him also reviled him" (Matthew 27:41–44).

But God remained silent and darkness covered the earth from the sixth to the ninth hour. There was physical anguish, but it was the mental, spiritual anguish which hurt most, the awareness of the separation brought about by sin, the isolation brought about by it. And Jesus is a lightning conductor, drawing the sin of the world down into his body, into the very fibres of his being.

Oh, man's capacity
For spiritual sorrow, corporal pain!
Who has explored the deepmost of that sea,
With heavy links of a far-fathoming chain?

That melancholy lead,
Let down in guilty and in innocent hold,
Yet into childish hands delivered,
Leaves the sequestered floor, unreached, untold.

One only has explored
The deepmost; but He did not die of it.
Not yet, not yet He died. Man's human Lord
Touched the extreme; it is not infinite.

But over the abyss
Of God's capacity for woe He stayed
One hesitating hour; what gulf was this?
Forsaken He went down, and was afraid.

("The Crucifixion", by Alice Meynell)

The mystery is that the trial and the disaster had fallen not on a sinner but on one who had called on God from his birth. "When Christ came into the world", says the writer of the Letter to the Hebrews, "he said, 'Lo, I have come to do your will, O God'" (10:5, 7). Or as the psalm Jesus was praying put it:

Yes, it was you who took me from the womb,
entrusted me to my mother's breast.
To you I was committed from my birth,
from my mother's womb you have been my God.
Do not leave me alone in my distress;
come close, there is none else to help . . .

Like water I am poured out,
disjointed are all my bones.

> *My heart has become like wax,*
> *it is melted within my breast.*
> *Parched as burnt clay is my throat,*
> *my tongue cleaves to my jaws.*
>
> *Many dogs have surrounded me,*
> *a band of the wicked beset me.*
> *They tear holes in my hands and my feet*
> *and lay me in the dust of death.*
>
> *I can count every one of my bones.*
> *These people stare at me and gloat;*
> *they divide my clothing among them.*
> *They cast lots for my robe.*

(Psalm 21)

The mystery for the Christian is that we are here face to face with a God who self-emptied himself in order to be completely human, whose heart melts like wax. "Though he was in the form of God, he did not count equality with God a thing to be grasped, but emptied himself, taking the form of a servant, being born in the likeness of men. And being found in human form he humbled himself and became obedient unto death, even death on a cross" (Philippians 2:6–8).

Michel Quoist puts it in contemporary terms in his *Prayers of Life*:

> *I am living flesh, throbbing, suffering.*
> *I am among men, and they have not recognized me.*
> *I am poorly paid, I am unemployed, I live in a*
> *   slum, I have tuberculosis, I sleep under*
> *   bridges, am in prison, I am oppressed, I am*
> *   patronized . . .*
> *They are scourging me, crucifying me,*
> *They tear me apart when they tear at one another.*
> *They kill me when they kill one another.*
> *(from "Son, I beseech you, don't sleep any more")*

This is important – to realize that though God came to us at a certain point in history, that Jesus was crucified on a particular Friday, his entry is indeed timeless, and when a man or a woman made in God's image is suffering, God is suffering. It was, I think, the Swedish Archbishop Söderblom who wrote somewhere that the unbeliever says, "If God existed he couldn't look on the sufferings and agony of man and live, his heart would break." And the crucifix answers, "God's heart *did* break."

6. *Seven Words from the Cross*

As I come before the cross of Jesus I come "burdened": a sudden death last week leaving a widow for whom I have felt deeply; a dear friend in danger of losing the baby she is carrying; a lady badly burned and struggling to remake her life; all the sadness of conflict in the Middle East. I have just been reading Doris Lessing's powerful and painful stories of Africa, to say nothing of my own personal worries and the burden of my own sin – with all this I come "burdened" before the cross of Jesus.

I can't in all seriousness maintain that my personal crosses are of the kind that would make me cry out, "My God, my God, why have you forsaken me?" Indeed, I often feel like a spoilt child of God, I have so little to suffer. But coming to the cross I bear with me the despair of others who feel that God has deserted them and who see their own feelings mirrored in that cry of dereliction of the child of God, the servant of God, the Son of God, calling to his Father, "Why have you forsaken me?"

What a mystery is here! What guilt must he be carrying to cause such a cry! What burden does he bring to Golgotha!

"Surely he has borne our griefs and carried our sorrows – upon him was the chastisement that made us whole – cut off out of the land of the living, stricken for the transgression of his people" (Isaiah 53:4, 5, 8). And he calls to himself all who are burdened: "Come to me, all who labour and are heavy burdened", calls them to share the mystery, the secret of the cross.

As Jesus hung on the cross his arms were stretched wide to embrace the whole world; and for *all* – men and women, good and evil, sinners and saints, nuns and whores, priests and pimps, young and old, rich and poor, black and white and yellow – for all he offered himself in a profound prayer which was the giving of himself, of his whole self, to the Father. "Seven times he spoke – seven words of love – and all three hours his silence cried – for mercy on the souls of men – Jesus our Lord is crucified."

1. **There they crucified him . . . and Jesus said, "Father, forgive them: for they know not what they do"** (Luke 23:33–34).

Is this perhaps the first awareness we must have, we who so readily fall into sin, that we must beware of judging others? It is very easy, when we read of this or that act of violence in our society, to rise in righteous anger and indignation, though it is perhaps not always quite so righteous as it might at first sight appear to be. The first stone is always the easiest to throw – but then one has to realize that it *is* the first stone. It is not that we should condone sin and evil, only that when we do judge we must remember that we also are sinners, and that we are quite capable of our own particular brand of violence. That is the language of the Sermon on the Mount, and desperately hard to put into practice. On the cross we see Jesus practising what he preached.

2. **The dying robber said to him, "Lord, remember me when you come into your kingdom." And Jesus said to him, "Truly, I say to you, today you will be with me in Paradise"** (Luke 23:42–43).

"The sinner", Péguy wrote, "stands at the very heart of Christendom." Here at the cross, next to the cross of Jesus, the very first to benefit from the redeeming power which Jesus won on Calvary, was the archetypal thug, the robbery-with-violence man, the grievous-bodily-harm thief; and the violence of the criminal meets up with the love of God.

Again, it is not a question of condoning sin – the thief was a repentant thief – but the love of Jesus, our model, went out to him "while he was yet a sinner" (cf. Romans 5:8), and this thug became the first one to enter through the gate flung wide open by Christ's death.

Can we remember just this: our common humanity? We can't shrug off our blood relationship with all men and women. We cannot shrug off our common heritage of sin, we are all in it together.

Dostoevsky makes his holy man, the Staretz Zossima, say, "He must realize that he is not only worse than others but that he is responsible to all men for all and everything, for all human sins, national and individual . . . every one of us, dear ones, is undoubtedly responsible for all men and everything on earth . . . not merely through the general sinfulness of creation, but each one personally for all mankind and each individual man . . . only through that knowledge our heart grows soft with infinite, universal, inexhaustible love. Then every one of you will have the power to win over the whole world by love and to wash away the sins of the world with your tears."

3. **When Jesus saw his mother, and the disciple whom he loved standing near, he said to his mother, "Woman, behold your son!" Then he said to the disciple, "Behold your mother!"** (John 19:26–27).

We remember the words of Jesus during his ministry, "Who are my mother and my brothers? Whoever does the will of God is my brother, and sister, and mother" (Mark 3:33, 35).

We are reminded too of the parable of the sheep and the goats, "as you did it to one of the least of these my brethren, you did it to me" (Matthew 25:40).

Violence is done to *him.* The violence in Northern Ireland or in the Middle East is a continuing passion, a continuing crucifixion of Christ. The violence of our society, whether that means profitable concerns making profits from underpaid workers in Africa, or the office manager who bullies some young typist into tears, or the "I'm all right, Jack" attitude, this violence is done to Christ. It is Christ who is reduced to tears, Christ who is undernourished, Christ who is left to get by as best he can with what is left over. "Behold your mother."

4. And at the ninth hour Jesus cried with a loud voice, "Eloi, Eloi, lama sabachthani?" which means, "My God, my God, why have you forsaken me?" (Mark 15:34).

Christ entered the depths. He plumbed depths lower than any we can discover – but nevertheless, if we follow him down in our prayers, in those depths, in that dereliction, in that despair of utter loneliness and abandonment, we meet the wrecks of violence in our society, the victims of man's aggressiveness to man, man's unconcern for man.

5. After this Jesus, knowing that all was now achieved, said (to fulfil the scripture), "I thirst" (John 19:28).

Jesus had always thirsted after the will of God, had always thirsted after righteousness – indeed it was that thirst which had brought him to the cross. That thirst continued and continues ever since. But on the cross, whatever spiritual significance we may – as St John did – choose to read into it, he *literally* was parched, physically parched with thirst.

And there are in our society, in our world, men, women and children who are necessarily so preoccupied with hungering and thirsting after their ordinary daily sustenance that they can't even begin to get round to hungering and thirsting after things of the spirit. We may not live where this can be seen daily on the streets, but we are constantly reminded of it by photographs in our newspapers. We have to remember what Jesus said on another occasion: "I was thirsty and you gave me drink" (Matthew 25:35). A society which spends millions of pounds on luxuries or on armaments whilst hundreds of thousands of Christ's brothers and sisters die of hunger has not yet heard – really heard – that voice croaking from the cross.

6. When Jesus had received the vinegar, he said, "It is achieved"; and he bowed his head and gave up his spirit (John 19:30).

All our prayer is founded on the certainty that God's will prevails. If we dare to face up to the monstrosities of our society, the sham and façades which hide rottenness within, the godlessness within, we can do so without despair because the victory is with the cross. We can put our backs into changing our society because we believe that the end is not blackness and despair and oblivion. Because the victory on the cross was *achieved*, we have become servants of a kingdom which in the end will win out.

7. It was now about the sixth hour, and there was darkness over the whole land until the ninth hour, while the sun's light failed; and the curtain of the temple was torn in two. Then Jesus, crying with a loud voice, said, "Father, into thy hands I commit my spirit!" (Luke 23:44–46).

These reflections began with the realization that we are not godly beings looking down from on high upon wicked people with whom we have nothing in common, over whom we can tut-tut. We are of one flesh with all sinners.

When we pray for that wounded body which is violent, unjust, obscene twentieth-century humanity, we are praying for ourselves, for our sick selves. We call out for God's mercy, "Father, forgive US, for we know not what we do." And we end, as Jesus did, by putting everything into the hands of the Father.

7. *Life Through Death*

I once met a man who, as a political deviant, had for four years undergone "psychiatric" treatment in a Soviet mental hospital. He was a Jew with no very religious ideas, but a profoundly human person whose patient endurance mirrored the Jesus pattern and whose spirit was quite unbroken. I recall indeed the bishop who ordained me a priest, a Soviet citizen who had been secretly consecrated in Moscow back in the 1920s. He was eventually picked up by the OGPU (the Soviet police and secret police from 1923 to 1934), spent twelve years in labour camps in Siberia and four more in the Arctic Circle, and he had indeed tasted the depths. I marvelled at the victory of the Russian Jew over his persecutors. I know that my bishop came through to a transparent goodness and meekness which meant that he, and not the commissars, had won. And I think of Jesus who accepted the obedience unto death, and *therefore* God highly exalted him and gave him the name which is above all others. Jesus so totally accepted, that he was totally the victor and therefore totally liberated from every limitation of the human condition. It was that total acceptance that won the victory – "Was it not necessary that the Christ should suffer these things and enter into his glory?" (Luke 24:26). What we see on the cross is total obedience, total trust. On the previous night in the Garden of Gethsemane he had prayed, "Father, if it is possible let this cup pass me by". He had seen the abyss of dereliction into which he must go. "Nevertheless, not my will, but your will be done."

The Father always listened to his Son, and heard his prayer. The answer came on Easter morning: because he loved, because he trusted, he conquered.

O Lord, do not leave me alone,
my strength, make haste to help me.
Rescue my soul from the sword,
my life from the grip of these dogs.
Save my life from the jaws of these lions,
my poor soul from the horns of these oxen.
I will tell of your name to my brethren
and praise you where they are assembled.
You who fear the Lord, give him praise;
all sons of Jacob, give him glory.
Revere him, Israel's sons.
For he has never despised
nor scorned the poverty of the poor.
From him he has not hidden his face,
but he heard the poor man when he cried.

(Psalm 21)

As Jesus draws to the close of the psalm which had begun so terrifyingly, his life is ebbing away and he can affirm with all the love of his heart, "Father," – so safely, so confidently – "into your hands I commend my spirit."

We can dismiss totally from our minds any notion of a Father and Son at variance – Father demanding, Son rebelling; Father exacting, Son reluctantly giving. The relationship of Father and Son is a relationship of love. From that relationship crucified was to come that Spirit of Love which Jesus could give to us only after he had been glorified, that is to say, after he had been crucified. He came to "bring gifts to men" and the Spirit was his great gift.

There is a lovely poem of George Herbert's about the dying Christ who gives:

> *Having been tenant long to a rich Lord,*
> *Not thriving, I resolved to be bold,*
> *And make a suit unto him, to afford*
> *A new small-rented lease, and cancel the old.*

> *In heaven at his manor I him sought:*
> *They told me there, that he was lately gone*
> *About some land, which he had dearly bought*
> *Long since on earth, to take possession.*
> *I straight returned, and knowing his great birth,*
> *Sought him accordingly in great resorts:*
> *In cities, theatres, gardens, parks and courts.*
> *At length I heard a ragged noise and mirth*
> *Of thieves and murderers: there I him espied,*
> *Who straight, Your suit is granted, said, and died.*
> ("Redemption")

Small wonder that Christians who have experienced his gift want so much to give to him in return, knowing all the time that what they can give is as nothing compared to his total giving.

> *Were the whole realm of nature mine,*
> *That were an offering far too small;*
> *Love so amazing, so divine,*
> *Demands my soul, my life, my all.*

"That young prince of glory" (Isaac Watts's original words), the young Victor, the Hero, has through the centuries been a Christian insight into the real meaning of the cross. From Clement of Alexandria we hear: "Let us hasten, let us run, we who are images of the Word, beloved of God and made in his likeness, let us love Christ, the noble charioteer of men. He led the foal and its parent under the same yoke and now having yoked together the team of mankind he shapes the course of his chariot for the goal of immortality. He drove first into Jerusalem, but now in heaven, a most notable spectacle for the Father, the eternal Son bringing the victory!"

From Clement of Alexandria in the second to third centuries to Sydney Carter's "Lord of the Dance", which tells of the Word of God dancing to earth at Bethlehem:

I danced in the morning when the world was begun,
And I danced in the moon and the stars and the sun.
And I came down from heaven and I danced on the
  earth —
At Bethlehem I had my birth . . .

They whipped and they stripped and they hung me
  on high
And they left me there on a cross to die.

I danced on a Friday when the sky turned black —
It's hard to dance with the devil on your back;
They buried my body and they thought I'd gone —
But I am the Dance and I still go on.

They cut me down and I leap up high.
I am the Life that'll never, never die.
I'll live in you if you'll live in me,
I am the Lord of the Dance, said he.

The Dancing Christ of Sydney Carter is the airy Christ of
Stevie Smith's poem:

Who is this that comes in splendour, coming from
  the blazing East?
This is he we had not thought of, this is he, the airy
  Christ.

Airy, in an airy manner in an airy parkland
  walking,
Others take him by the hand, lead him, do the
  talking.

But the Form, the airy One, frowns an airy frown,
What they say he knows must be, but he looks
  aloofly down,

Looks aloofly at his feet, looks aloofly at his hands,
Knows they must, as prophets say, nailèd be to
    wooden bands.

As he knows the words he sings, that he sings so
    happily
Must be changed to working laws, yet sings he
    ceaselessly.

Those who truly hear the voice, the words, the
    happy song,
Never shall need working laws to keep from doing
    wrong.

Deaf men will pretend sometimes they hear the
    song, the words,
And make excuse to sin extremely; this will be
    asbsurd.

Heed it not. Whatever foolish men may do the
    song is cried
For those who hear, and the sweet singer does not
    care that he was crucified.

For he does not wish that men should love him
    more than anything
Because he died; he only wishes they would hear
    him sing.

For as Jesus said in a last triumphant cry, "It is accomplished!" Not the "It's all over, thank God" of a tired and exhausted man, but a triumphant, exultant "I have accomplished it. I have achieved what I set out to do. I've been into the depths and I've won!" The power of evil had done its worst and, like waves beating against a granite rock, the power of Evil had been resisted and defeated. Indeed, more than that, as the Byzantines have loved to portray it, Christ had kicked in the doors of Hades which cannot stand up against him.

So what of us? We don't need to apportion blame. Certainly not to the Jewish people. But for us there is surely repentance.

> *Drop, drop, slow tears,*
> *And bathe those beauteous feet,*
> *Which brought from heaven*
> *The news and Prince of Peace.*
>
> *Cease not, wet eyes,*
> *His mercies to entreat;*
> *To cry for vengeance*
> *Sin doth never cease.*
>
> *In your deep floods*
> *Drown all my faults and fears;*
> *Nor let his eye*
> *See sin, but through my tears.*
>
> ("A Hymn", by Phineas Fletcher)

> *"My people, what have I done to you?*
> *How have I offended you? Answer me!"*
> (from the "Reproaches" of the Good Friday liturgy)

Repentance, yes, but above all confidence in his forgiveness, forgiveness of everything, sins of youth, sins of middle age, and also our final sin. Can I call John Donne to witness:

> *Wilt thou forgive that sin where I begun,*
> *Which is my sin, though it were done before?*
> *Wilt thou forgive those sins through which I run,*
> *And do them still, though I do still deplore?*
> *When thou hast done, thou hast not done,*
> *For I have more.*

> *Wilt thou forgive that sin by which I won*
> *Others to sin, and made my sin their door?*
> *Wilt thou forgive that sin which I did shun*
> *A year or two, but wallowed in a score?*
> *When thou hast done, thou hast not done,*
> *For I have more.*
>
> *I have a sin of fear, that when I've spun*
> *My last thread, I shall perish on the shore;*
> *Swear by thyself that at my death thy Sun*
> *Shall shine as it shines now, and heretofore;*
> *And having done that, thou hast done,*
> *I have no more.*
>
> ("A Hymn to God the Father")

And there is the knowledge that, joined to his agony, our agonies can share in his redeeming, saving work, and like him we trust, and like him we love, and like him we give. And there is the sure hope that in him we can conquer, even our final enemy, Death. Death which is the ultimate obstacle in man's attempt to be himself without God, the ultimate consequence of sin, death in the cross of Jesus becomes instead the gateway to life. I look forward to the resurrection of the dead! Jesus opened up the path on Good Friday. I have nothing to fear. This is not a God who came slumming and then got back as fast as he could to his luxury heaven. He came and suffered and died in this way because that is the way he is. When I see Jesus on the cross I have a truer picture of the real God than seeing him with all the trappings of glory. I see the heart of God; and of such a loving God I need have no fear. I do have no fear. I am simply, humbly grateful. We adore you, O Christ, and we bless you, because by your precious blood you have redeemed the world!

8. *The Easter Victory*

When Jesus met his disciples on the evening of his resurrection day, his greeting was "*Shalom* – Peace!" Their hearts were troubled, not only because of the death of Jesus and the end of their hopes, not only because they were doubtful now as to whether they were seeing a ghost (though they'd had that fright once before on the Sea of Galilee), but troubled because two days ago they had let him down, failed him, deserted him in his hour of trial. Their leader had even denied that he knew him. So they had "bad consciences". And now Jesus comes towards them with that word full of consolation: "*Shalom* – Peace be with you! Be at peace!" And we too as we reflect on our own letting down of him, our own betrayals of him, of his way, of his ideals, of his message (and indeed our betrayal of each other, of one another's trust), we can hear that word of Jesus steal quietly into our hearts: "*Shalom*! Be at peace!"

Look again at St John's description of that resurrection appearance of Jesus as he tells it in his twentieth chapter, and see how Jesus passes on that message of peace and reconciliation to us and *through* us:

> On the evening of that day, the first day of the week, the doors being shut where the disciples were, for fear of the Jews, Jesus came and stood among them and said to them, "Peace be with you." When he had said this, he showed them his hands and his side. Then the disciples were glad when they saw the Lord. Jesus said to them again, "Peace be with you. As the Father has sent me, even so I send you." And when he had said this, he breathed on

> **them, and said to them, "Receive the Holy Spirit.
> If you forgive the sins of any, they are forgiven; if
> you retain the sins of any, they are retained"**
> (20:19–23).

It was beautifully taken up hundreds of years later, in the
sixteenth century, by Edmund Spenser:

> *Most glorious Lord of life, that on this day*
> *Didst make thy triumph over death and sin;*
> *And having harrowed hell didst bring away*
> *Captivity thence captive, us to win:*
> *This joyous day, dear Lord, with joy begin,*
> *And grant that we for whom thou diddest die*
> *Being with thy dear blood clean washed from sin,*
> *May live for ever in felicity.*
>
> *And that thy love we weighing worthily,*
> *May likewise love thee for the same again;*
> *And for thy sake that all like dear didst buy,*
> *With love may one another entertain.*
> *So let us love, dear love, like as we ought.*
> *Love is the lesson which the Lord us taught.*

The Easter story is, in fact, the most compelling evidence
for the often repeated, but not always credible, assertion
that love is indestructible: because the Jesus who rose from
the dead on Easter Day was the triumph of Love over
Death. The love which had taken him to the cross, and kept
him on it, that love was so powerful that it was incapable
of extinction and it carried Jesus triumphantly through to
the glories of Easter Day.

So if you, having loved, or loving, have an inkling that
that love cannot be destroyed, that it can leap over barriers
and frontiers, you are (though this may be an odd way of
putting it) dead right, and Easter says you are right.

The HOW is mystery, hidden in silence. You may know Alice Meynell's poem:

> *All night had shout of men and cry*
> *   Of woeful women filled his way;*
> *Until that noon of sombre sky*
> *   On Friday, clamour and display*
> *Smote him; no solitude had he,*
> *No silence, since Gethsemane.*
>
> *Public was Death; but Power, but Might,*
> *   But Life again, but Victory,*
> *Were hushed within the dead of night,*
> *   The shuttered dark, the secrecy.*
> *And all alone, alone, alone,*
> *He rose again behind the stone.*
>
> ("Easter Night")

Yes, love is discreet, humble and powerful. Love has the victory. When Roman Catholics gather on Easter night for their vigil in order to give thanks ("make Eucharist") for the resurrection of the Lord Jesus, all the strands which run through the whole story of man's relationship with God are gathered in the readings from the scriptures. It is a story of love, and that means that it is a costly, demanding story. It begins with the creation of the world, created by God, we believe, out of the munificence of his love, out of the sheer exuberance of it. It was love that brought everything into being: sun, moon, stars, earth, sky, sea, plants, fish, birds, animals and MAN and WOMAN. And when God had made it, he saw all that he had made and it was very good. The world came from God, our world, and it was good! It is important to remember that starting point – our world came out from the love of God as something good.

And then – and how well we know it – in a world that has somehow gone wrong, where it somehow hasn't worked out as it should, the great figures and events of the story are recalled: Abraham, man of faith and trust, man of real obedience to God, of real love for God; Moses, the friend of God, who led God's people out of slavery in Egypt towards the Promised Land in an Exodus which was to be for Christians the pattern of liberation, the foreshadowing of the great liberation from slavery to sin and death which was to come; the prophets, such as Ezekiel and Baruch, who told of a love and a mercy in God which, as it created the world and mankind, would re-create – that the purposes of God would not be defeated by sin and that the victory would be with the almightiness of God's love.

And so to Jesus, sent into the world because God so loved it, to save the world. Jesus, whose life-style was love. What else could it be since he "came from God"? Jesus, whose talk was all of love and an urging of those who wished to be his disciples to love, to be loving. Jesus, who died from and out of love.

If you can see the whole process of creation as life surging out from God, the life-blood of God coursing through the veins of the world, then think of Jesus as a major artery of life-love: Jesus as an intensification of what it was all about; Jesus summing up; Jesus perfectly expressing; Jesus concentrating in his own person; Jesus being the peak achievement of all that the creation, of all that humanity is in God's plan. The whole enormous mystery of love took shape in the person of Jesus, the "perfect" man, man as God intended him to be.

The apparent tragedy of the cross is that this whole, huge thrust of life and love was killed, obliterated, executed.

But then, so unexpectedly – "O foolish men, and slow of heart to believe all that the prophets have spoken!" (Luke 23:25) – we learn that it is not blocked off, not obliterated, that the life-love is untamed, throbs on, it cannot be stifled, it cannot be stilled. Jesus is alive! The thrust, the life-force, which has been driving through creation from the beginning, is up and about!

Yet with a difference. For in the resurrection of Jesus the creation takes a huge leap forward, as the love-power of Jesus breaks through the time/space barriers and a new sort of man, the first man of a new creation, a new Adam, comes into being. The sort of humanity, the sort of world, the sort of creation that Jesus had hinted at, had sown, had fostered, had initiated, was now firmly and irrevocably planted. Not as a one-off, not as an event of the past, but as a present, actual, abiding reality, in our world, for always: a leaven in our midst. And if we believe, if we love, we are caught up in that indestructible, Easter, resurrection-life – the life of the Spirit, the Holy Spirit of Jesus released now into the world.

9. *The Spirit of Jesus*

From the time that he came into the world Jesus was "Spirit-filled". Mary was "found to be with child of the Holy Spirit" (Matthew 1:18), and Luke records the words of the angel: "The Holy Spirit will come upon you, and the power of the Most High will overshadow you; therefore the child to be born will be called holy, the Son of God" (Luke 1:35).

In the power and presence of the Holy Spirit there was in the man, Jesus of Nazareth, a divine indwelling. He, who at his baptism by John as "well-beloved Son" would be called holy, the Son of God, was anointed by the Holy Spirit. And then Jesus "full of the Holy Spirit . . . was led by the Spirit for forty days in the wilderness . . . and Jesus returned in the power of the Spirit into Galilee" (Luke 4:1–2, 14). It was that same Spirit which came upon him in the synagogue at Nazareth "to preach . . . to proclaim release . . . to give sight . . . to set at liberty"(Luke 4:18). And when he had passed through death he was, as St Paul says, "designated Son of God in power according to the Spirit of holiness by his resurrection from the dead" (Romans 1:4).

The whole person and life of Jesus of Nazareth was from conception to glory "Spirit-filled", and that eternal movement of love which is the very life of the Godhead, that whole movement within the Blessed Trinity which is the Holy Spirit, swept out in time in the Spirit-filled, love-filled son of Mary.

In all his actions Jesus is "in the Spirit" – his access to the Father is "in the Spirit". "In that same hour", the Gospel says, "he rejoiced in the Holy Spirit and said, 'I thank thee, Father, Lord of heaven and earth'" (Luke

10:21) – his obedience to the Father, his praise of the Father, is in the Holy Spirit.

And as a direct consequence of his cross and resurrection he hands on his Holy Spirit to us. On the cross he "gave up his spirit" to the Father ("Father, into thy hands I commend my spirit") and by the same act of giving he handed on his spirit to those who believe in him. "He breathed on them, and said unto them, 'Receive the Holy Spirit'" (John 20:22). This was a dramatic change – until then the Spirit-activity of Jesus was, so to say, confined to his personal actions and life, but now he was glorified, and "being therefore", as St Peter said in the first Christian sermon on the Day of Pentecost, "exalted at the right hand of God, and having received from the Father the promise of the Holy Spirit, *he has poured out this which you see and hear*" (Acts 2:33). Pentecost is the Paschal Mystery of Death and Resurrection brought to completion. Those who believe, those on whom the Spirit of the Risen Jesus is poured out, become "temples of the Holy Spirit" (cf. 1 Corinthians 6:19). And most important of all, "all who are led by the Spirit of God are sons of God. For you did not receive the spirit of slavery to fall back into fear, but you have received the spirit of sonship" (the very spirit of Jesus!). "When we cry Abba! Father! it is the Spirit himself bearing witness with our spirit that we are children of God, and if children, then heirs, heirs of God, and fellow heirs with Christ" (Romans 8:14–17). The terrifying, unapproachable God of the vision of Isaiah, "high and lifted up", becomes Abba. Planted in our fleshly nature is the new seed of the Spirit. There is in us something of Jesus.

Why on earth do you imagine you do the good things you do? It is the Spirit of Jesus within you. Why do you pray? It is the Spirit of Jesus praying within you. Why are you loving? It is the Spirit of Jesus loving within you. Yes, we have been given this glorious gift, the Spirit-power has been released within us. Don't let us deny the good that is within us – you can deny that it is anything of *ours*, but not deny that it exists or talk as though his Risen Power has done nothing.

At this stage the Spirit, it is true, is warring against the flesh, at this stage we have only the first fruits of the Spirit; we are still far from the Perfect Man, Man Perfected which we see in Jesus. But if we have been born again of water and the Spirit we know that we already have one leg cocked over the fence, that eternal life is already welling up within us, that there is a power to be free set loose within us. JESUS CAME TO SET US FREE! And it means, of course, that we are never alone – the battle is not that one-sided.

There is a lovely commentary of St Gregory the Great on that phrase in the Song of Songs, "Behold, he comes leaping on the mountains":

> **In the coming task of our redemption he made, if I may so speak, certain leaps. Do you desire, dearest brethren, to know what those leaps were?**
>
>> *From heaven he came down to a womb*
>> *from the womb to a crib*
>> *from the crib to a cross*
>> *from the cross to a tomb*
>> *from the tomb he returned to heaven.*
>
> **Behold how the Truth, made known in the flesh that he might induce us to run after him, made for us certain leaps: for he rejoiced as a giant to run the way, that we might from our hearts cry out to him, "Draw us after thee; we will run after thee in the odour of thy ointments." And for this, dearest brethren, we must follow him in our hearts . . . let us follow him with the footsteps of love. And he who gave us this love will not be indifferent to it, Jesus Christ our Lord.**

He calls us, as he called those Galilean fishermen of old, to follow him in his way of love. In the end all the other things will pass away – popes and priests, sacraments and laws – in the end love alone remains in an eternal Easter. And to be there, we must follow him. If we search we shall find and he is the Way.

10. *About Prayer*

There are three points I would like to make: first, that people are often on the path of prayer without realizing it; secondly, that even a busy day can give us all sorts of opportunities for very real prayer; and thirdly, that we shouldn't lose heart if we feel that, prayer-wise, we have wasted a day.

I was once talking with someone who had a problem about prayer. She had just come to us by bus, it was a beautiful sunny day and she had been thinking exactly that: "What a lovely day it is!" In my opinion she was already on the path of prayer. She could of course have said: "Thank you, God! What a lovely day it is!" and that would have sharpened it up a bit. She could have said with the psalmist: "The heavens declare the glory of God" and that too would have sharpened it up. She could have said – as Tertullian, back in the second century, used to say when he saw the birds flying in the sky with their wings outstretched – that they were all praising God and making the sign of the cross – have a look next time, because they really do. The very fact that you marvel at a flower, or a girl, or a mountain, or a beautiful act of kindness – if you are marvelling, if you have an experience of wonder, however brief – you are on the threshold of prayer. So, busy person that you may be, don't too quickly downgrade your prayer capacity, because that path of wonder is surely the way to God – a sense of wonder at the wonderfulness of people, of things, of very ordinary things. Brother Lawrence, who lived in the presence of God among the pots and pans of the kitchen and whose experience led to the book *The Practice of the Presence of God*, could "exult in the Lord" as he made the stew. If we are "aware", when we are aware, the soul is on the path to God. Prayer is a matter of being more aware, of being more ready still to lift up one's heart.

Some years ago in a broadcast I talked about two marvellous gasometers on the North Circular Road around London, the sight of which always lifted my heart when I went past them, and that is still true – the sight of their lacelike crowns still makes me marvel. But I could say the same of the stallholders in the market where I shop for vegetables – their cheerful friendliness "lifts up my heart" and I think of the wonder that is God. When that happens to me that is prayer – I catch a glimpse of God. He is so beautiful and he radiates this beauty into our lives so marvellously and so many-splendouredly (I think of the beauty of the loving trustfulness of someone recently bereaved – oh, in so many ways), and if I respond wonderingly and gratefully that is prayer, a window on God. And that is a prayer that can grow and become part of me and you, a movement of my spirit and your spirit towards God.

Brother Lawrence, who really lived in the presence of God, dated his conversion at the age of eighteen from something totally simple. We are told, "In the winter, seeing a tree stripped of its leaves and considering that in a little time the leaves would be renewed and after that the flowers and fruit appear, he received a high view of the providence and power of God which has never since been effaced from his soul."

But though it is true that a wondering response to people, to things, to events that crowd in on us in a busy day can allow God to break into our lives, nevertheless that very busy-ness can push any direct Me–God talk out of our hearts. I live in a monastery with a regular round of prayer times, I am surrounded by religious books and pictures, and yet I know only too well how, even with all that to help me, the time can slip by without my raising my mind to

God. Hopefully my heart has not strayed, but my mind, yes. And I am privileged. It is true that there is the door bell and the telephone, but I don't have to be concerned with babies or a thousand pressures to which other people are subject. So I appreciate that there are problems about any consistent "turning to God" throughout the day.

Even so, there are all sorts of ways in which the day does give us, presents to us, opportunities to pray. The door bell rings and it is very easy to say "Drat it!" – St Benedict, on the other hand, in his Rule for Monks, says this about the monk who has to answer the door: "As soon as anyone shall knock, or a poor person shall beg for charity, he shall say [not, 'Drat it'] 'Thanks be to God' or 'God bless you', and then with all the gentleness of the fear of God, let him quickly respond in the fervour of charity." There's a whole prayer pattern for telephonists and receptionists! In the bus or tube it is, in fact, just as easy, instead of reading the advertisements, to pray over the person sitting opposite you, who won't be at all aware of what you are up to (I find this great fun!), won't realize that for the last five minutes you have been calling down God's blessing on him or her, their family, their work, their happiness, their health.

There is a great Jewish tradition of prayer for all circumstances – the blessing of God at all times and in all places (the tradition in which Jesus the Jew grew up). I'm sure a lot of people would be astonished at the very thought that time in the loo is a good opportunity for prayer – it sounds rather improper and not quite nice; but why not? A little spiritual classic by a monk of the Eastern Church suggests among other things that when we are washing we have a marvellous occasion for a brief dart of prayer: "Wash me, Lord; if you wash me, Lord, I shall be really clean."

It is a very ancient prayer pattern, constantly recommended by the spiritual masters, to dart little prayers towards God at any time of the day (or of the night, if you can't sleep). They can be as brief as one single word: "Lord", or (and this has a very hallowed tradition behind it): "Lord Jesus Christ, Son of the Living God, be merciful to me, a sinner." As Brother Lawrence said: "A little lifting up of the heart suffices; a little remembrance of God, one act of inward worship, are prayers which, however short, are nevertheless very acceptable to God."

"Be merciful to me, a sinner" – I'm going to say something I'm sure will be misunderstood, but I am going to say it, so let me preface it by saying precisely that. The one *good* thing about sin is that when we have sinned we are able to recognize what we are, we are humbled before God. One really big sin in one's life has this to be said in its favour, that it is an excellent way of coming to a true awareness of one's frailty and one's total dependence on God's grace, that we depend on God for our salvation and not on ourselves. Don't misunderstand me. I'm not (repeat, NOT) saying, "Go out today and commit a really good sin and this will then be an occasion to learn the prayer of humility." But I am saying that when we have sinned grossly it is a marvellous way to learn "humble prayer".

As a Roman Catholic, the one thing I really envy the Church of England is that prayer in the Book of Common Prayer called "The Prayer of Humble Access". You are perhaps familiar with it: "We do not presume to come to this thy table, O Merciful Lord, trusting in our own righteousness, but in thy manifold and great mercies. We are not worthy so much as to gather up the crumbs under thy table: but thou art the same Lord, whose property is always to have mercy."

Of Brother Lawrence, who practised constant awareness of God's presence, we are told that when he failed in his duty he only confessed his fault saying to God, "If you leave me to myself I will never do otherwise; you have to prevent my falling and put right what is amiss", and after this he gave himself no uneasiness about it.

So I would like to suggest, busy you, that you try to find some time in the course of the day for the prayer of humility. And, and this is very important, if you have had a day wasted as far as prayer is concerned, if you have to say, "Yesterday I didn't pray at all", don't despair. Make of it a grace. If it means that your prayer now begins "Lord, I am not worthy", then that prayerless day will not have been wasted. We are weak, we do fail in our good intentions, we are frail. And our very recognition of that is already prayer.

You will recall the story Jesus told of the publican and the pharisee. The pharisee was able to tell God just how good he, the pharisee, was (not how good God was) – he really did say his prayers not only every day, but all day. The publican didn't dare even to lift his eyes from the ground: he was so conscious of the shameful, God-forgetting life he led, and all he could manage to say was, "Be merciful to me, a sinner." And what was Jesus's comment? This man went down to his house justified – right with God. But then who am I to be talking to you about prayer, feeble that mine is? Only last weekend it went for a burton. But if, like me, you feel that yours is feeble; if in your busy life prayer has got crowded out, join me in saying, somewhere, sometime, in today's busy-ness, "Lord, be merciful to me, a sinner." After that we really can say, "Over to you, God."

11. *More About Prayer*

I no longer live near those gasometers which lifted my heart. Instead I live in Bedfordshire near brickworks, with a forest of tall chimneys which remind me of an Italian city of mediaeval towers, and the sight of them gives me a spiritual kick too. Lots of things can do that, put that zip into our hearts and make us want to say "Great!", and if the next stage is "Great, God!" we are well on the path of prayer.

Isn't there a song (or was it an old mission hymn?) which has a refrain of "Count your blessings one by one"? Love and warmth, sunlight and devoted nursing, children and fun, there are a host of things for which one wants to say thank you.

I think that I'm not very grateful, in that I take an awful lot for granted. I take my very existence for granted, but I need to thank the Lord for the wonder of my being, for those who brought me into the world, who cared for me as a child, who sacrificed themselves for me. I need to thank the Lord for the good world around me, for all the good things he has given us on this earth of ours. I need to say thank you for love and friendship, for forgiveness and understanding granted when I have made a fool of myself.

Life is a great mixture of ups and downs. My life is a mixture of doubts and certainties, of joys and sorrows. I need to know how to sing his praise not only when I'm on top of the world, but also when I'm feeling blue.

John Newton, the slave trader, had a conversion experience which gave him a knowledge of the living Jesus, he knew Jesus as someone for real in his life, and out of the reality of that experience he wrote not only about the "Amazing grace that saved a wretch like me", but also a hymn with the lines, "Come, my soul, thy suit prepare, Jesus loves to answer prayer". When we come to prayer we come to someONE, and that someone is one "whose grace and power are such, None can ever ask too much".

We come, all of us, needing God's pardon and each other's pardon, and we are all in the same boat, carrying the burden of our sins and failures. (The only person I have ever met who really thought she was without sin also told me she thought I had beautiful feet – you will gather she was rather odd.) No, we come, all of us, needing pardon. We come forgiving as we trust to be forgiven. Our awareness of this drives us to our knees. What is not on – how could it be? – is any pretence! If God is for real he knows me even better than I know myself, much better than I know myself. And the extraordinary thing about this extraordinary God is that he accepts me as I am, for what I am.

So I don't need to pretend, I don't need to explain, I don't need to try to justify myself (I can't anyway), all I need to do is to recognize myself for what I am and say that I am sorry, that I repent. I come asking for forgiveness knowing, in Newton's words, that I can never ask too much. I think that is fantastic; not fantastic because a fantasy, but fantastically marvellous. The one person before whom I don't need to put up any front, the one person before whom I *can't* put up any front, before whom I stand quite naked, LOVES me and accepts me. Before God I am "in the truth" and I am not turned away. He actually loves me, and if that is what prayer is all about, I am getting somewhere. But there is a snag. Someone is not very happy with the situation. You've guessed – the devil! If he can stop me coming to that point of repentant, grateful, praiseful, loving, trusting union with God, he will do his damnedest. It is the theme of C. S. Lewis's classic *Screwtape Letters* – taking prayer seriously is a devilish disaster.

Now I do realize that it is a very dicey thing to make large, generalized statements about the way people pray or should pray. Each of us has our own unique prayer relationship with God. But there is one obvious danger for all of us – and that is the danger of praying as we *were*. That is to say that at the age of 18 or 28 or 68 or whatever, to be still talking baby language. I did once know someone who at the age of 35 was still praying the language of "Gentle Jesus, meek and mild, look upon this little child" (which she had, of course, long since ceased to be). The prayer I make has to be *my* prayer, me as I am now.

Screwtape's other weapon was to get people to realize that, and then to launch them into a sort of prayer cloud-cuckoo land. There is a real "prayer of quiet" when one is simply there before the Lord. You have probably heard of the old man who used to sit still in church saying nothing, and then when he was quizzed about it said, "I just look at him and he looks at me" – that is a very high form of prayer, not at all the same thing as being all vague and bleary. It implies a high form of concentration and yet is in fact very relaxed.

But a lot of us don't live on Cloud Nine, so there is a lot to be said for developing a prayer vocabulary. The psalmist, for instance, can provide us with plenty, and a prayer book may be a great help – but it's better still to make one's own prayer book.

There has too to be a certain discipline. We don't always feel on top of the world, we do get colds, we do feel tired and so we are tempted to say, "Oh, well, today I'll skip it, I don't feel like it!" Believe me, that happens to the professionals (vicars and monks, bishops and nuns, the lot) just as much as to anyone else. So a certain sticking at it, a certain perseverance is terribly important. We can pray anywhere but we are more likely to if we have a firm base. Of course, I can pray in the bus, but I'm more likely to do that if there is also time in my day which is actually set apart for prayer, when I sit or kneel (it doesn't matter which as long as it isn't sloppy) and recognize the Presence. Words can help (some phrase from the Bible), pictures can help, but always beyond the words and images we must remember that it is God we are with, God we are after, and God we will want to listen to. Prayer is not me talking all the time, but me placed at God's disposal.

One of the mistakes we often make when we are thinking about prayer is to suppose that we have to do all the work, that in some way it is something that we create. It would be much truer to say that it is something God's Spirit creates in us, the Spirit without whom nothing exists anyway ("You send forth your Spirit and they are created", says the psalmist in Psalm 103). The Spirit of God is within us, waiting to set us on fire; what we mustn't do is to put an asbestos fire blanket over the flame which is ready to blaze up. It is the Spirit who turns prayer from a chore into a delight; it is the Spirit who groans in supplication within us when life isn't a delight, when we are not a delight to ourselves.

It is very difficult to be open with someone you can't trust or don't trust. But in the ordinary human life and language of Jesus, I see and hear a God who loves like a father, and whose love, stronger than death, gives life to me. *That* I can trust. I can say about him, "He is my Rock, my Fortress." I can only be really honest about my faults with someone who I know loves me. We have a God who only wants to help us and our feeble efforts at prayer, and who will pray in us, and because I am met in prayer by a God who is constant in his love for me, I don't want to go off with the Enemy, *his* enemy. I want to get to the stage where I can say every day: "To you all honour, praise and glory and power." Cloud Nine? But what if now it is *for real*?

12. *Creatures Great and Small*

Millions know "All creatures great and small" as the title of a popular and hilarious TV series. And millions more know it as a line from a popular hymn:

> All things bright and beautiful,
> All creatures great and small,
> All things wise and wonderful,
> The Lord God made them all.

There are three creatures I would like to take as a starting point for prayer: the cat, the donkey and the dog.

I begin with the cat. Ours is, in the words of the Song of Songs, "black but comely", by name the Lord Mordaunt, after the family who used to live some centuries ago in the village of Turvey where our monastery is.

You may perhaps be a cat-hater – someone who is utterly repelled when a cat arches its back and insists on rubbing against your leg – if so, put aside your prejudice for a moment and reflect on some lines of D. H. Lawrence entitled "Pax". If you are a cat-lover you will get the point immediately:

> All that matters is to be at one with the living God
> to be a creature in the house of the God of life.
>
> Like a cat asleep on a chair
> at peace, in peace
> and at one with the master of the house, with the
>   mistress,
> at home, at home in the house of the living,

> *sleeping on the hearth, and yawning before the
>   fire.*
>
> *Sleeping on the hearth of the living world
> yawning at home before the fire of life
> feeling the presence of the living God
> like a great reassurance
> a deep calm in the heart
> a presence
> as of the master sitting at the board
> in his own and greater being,
> in the house of life.*

Because that is very important in prayer – to be able, like a cat, to relax "in the presence", to feel that "great reassurance". We come so often to prayer all worked up and buzzing with our own busy-ness. Someone has upset us, or we have upset someone. Things have gone wrong at work, or you have just come from a whale of a party – for whatever reason we are all tensed up, and we need to "let go" in order to be "at one with the living God", to come to that "deep calm in the heart" and simply to know that God IS, and, like that cat, to feel secure, to be unafraid, because one is "at home".

Early in the morning, if the day's rush is already upon us, that may not be so easy. On the other hand, if you are curled up in bed and the rush has not begun, that may be just the moment to be simply and briefly "still" and to feel the presence of the living God. If the day is already launched on its busy-ness, then try to find some time during the day, like a cat, to stop and yawn before the fire of life.

Mind you, our cat is not always relaxed – he can switch in a flash from total relaxation into electrifying energy and be up in a bound. But that is the point, isn't it? – the prayer of quiet is a launching pad for action.

Then take the donkey. The rector of our village church

has one – a strange animal! (the donkey, I mean, not the rector) – a ludicrous animal! You may perhaps know G. K. Chesterton's poem about it:

> *When fishes flew and forests walked*
> *And figs grew upon thorn,*
> *Some moment when the moon was blood*
> *Then surely I was born;*
>
> *With monstrous head and sickening cry*
> *And ears like errant wings,*
> *The devil's walking parody*
> *On all four-footed things.*
>
> *The tattered outlaw of the earth,*
> *Of ancient crooked will;*
> *Starve, scourge, deride me: I am dumb,*
> *I keep my secret still,*
>
> *Fools! For I also had my hour;*
> *One far fierce hour and sweet:*
> *There was a shout about my ears,*
> *And palms before my feet.*

("The Donkey")

Yes, as St Paul says, "God chose what is foolish in the world . . . God chose what is weak in the world . . . God chose what is low and despised in the world, even things that are not, to bring to nothing things that are" (1 Corinthians 1:27–28). Oh, what a donkey, we say of someone, and dismiss him; but not so fast . . .

Ours is not an age which rates Humility very highly – oh yes, the phoney humility of understatement which implies the very opposite ("I don't claim to be good, BUT . . . "). We tend to be a pushy, climbing lot. But real humility is the very basis of prayer. The man in the parable who went down to his house justified in the sight of God was not the one who prayed listing all his own good qualities, but the sinner who would not even lift his eyes to heaven and who beat his breast, saying: "God, be merciful to me, a sinner." It is our real awareness of what we are in the sight of God – the donkey – which alone makes our prayer real. The acceptance of the truth about ourselves is the only starting point for a real relationship with God.

If today we are about to say of someone, as we look down on him, "Oh, he's such a donkey", we should think twice, and better still realize that we all have something of the donkey in us, because if we don't God can't do very much with us.

There was a custom in the Middle Ages at the Christmas Mass for the ministers in some places to do a sort of dialogue representing the animals at the crib at the time of Christ's birth. It began with the cock crowing CHRISTUS NATUS EST! (Christ is born!), and the ox lowing UBI? (Where?), and the sheep answering, bleatingly, IN BETHLEHEM. But it was the donkey, the *donkey*, who said EAMUS, EAMUS! (Let's go, Let's go!) For the foolishness of God is wiser than men, and the weakness of God is stronger than men.

The cat, the donkey and now the dog. But unlike the cat and the donkey, which I have suggested as models for us in our approach to prayer, the dog is a different one. This is not the dog as us, but the dog as God himself, God the Hound of Heaven, God pursuing us, God bounding behind us.

If you have ever been chased by a large dog, not a little one snapping at your heels, but a great bounding type like a wolf-hound, you will remember the experience and what it is like to search for a way out. It happened to me once when I was a boy at school and had to deliver a message late one evening, and this enormous hound came bounding out of the dark after me.

In Francis Thompson's great poem "The Hound of Heaven", God is the Hound:

> *Still with unhurrying chase,*
> *And unperturbèd pace,*
> *Deliberate speed, majestic instancy,*
> *Came on the following Feet,*
> *And a Voice above their beat —*
> *"Naught shelters thee, who will not shelter Me."*

But though this bounding Hound may at first sight seem not to be "man's best friend", this is what he proves to be. The Hound of Heaven pursues us as, in the end desperately, we seek to escape up what are in fact blind alleys (all the ones we know), as we look for contentment or fulfilment in whatever the world has to offer.

> *I fled Him down the nights and down the days;*
> *I fled him down the arches of the years;*
> *I fled Him down the labyrinthine ways*
> *Of my own mind; and in the midst of tears*
> *I hid from Him, and under running laughter.*
> *Up vistaed hopes I sped;*
> *And shot, precipitated,*
> *Adown Titanic glooms of chasmed fears,*
> *From those strong Feet that followed, followed*
> *after.*
> *But with unhurrying chase,*
> *And unperturbèd pace,*
> *Deliberate speed, majestic instancy,*
> *They beat — and a Voice beat*
> *More instant than the Feet —*
> *"All things betray thee, who betrayest Me."*

And God does not give up the chase until he can finally corner us and then:

Yes, Lord, I Believe

> *Halts by me that footfall:*
> *Is my gloom, after all*
> *Shade of His hand, outstretched caressingly?*
> *"Ah, fondest, blindest, weakest,*
> *I am He Whom thou seekest!*
> *Thou dravest love from thee, who dravest Me."*

As we go about our day this Hound of Heaven, who really is "man's best friend", will be pursuing us. We may look for satisfaction in any number of things – in work, in love, in fun – but they are all blind alleys. And it is no use saying, "Good boy, get down, Rover!", because he won't – not this dog.

13.

Four "Moral" Travelogues

1. Norman Castles

You won't, I'm sure, take me too seriously if I say that I have recently become a bit of an expert on Norman castles. During the Easter holidays I usually take the "altar servers" for a day out – that is to say, the boys who have, especially during the elaborate ceremonies of Holy Week, performed their duties in the sanctuary. It's a way of saying "thank you" for work well done.

On this particular Easter we did a variety of things, including a visit to the London Museum of Horror, which they not unexpectedly, loved and where they behaved rather well. (Unlike the time in the restaurant when they started throwing peas at each other to my intense embarrassment, so that I offered the waitress an exceptionally large tip, which she – soft-hearted woman! – refused saying, "Spend it on the boys.") Anyway, on this occasion the major item was to go up the River Thames and visit the Tower (or Castle) of London. Incidentally, it is curious to discover what things do actually please – on one occasion it was riding in a taxi which proved the highlight of the day.

Well, we went into the Tower and I really tried for the first time to get clear in my mind the shape and the point of that jumble of buildings, and particularly of the Keep, the great White Tower. Then it so happened that about three weeks later I found myself at Rochester, where there are the remains of yet another castle and a fairly well-preserved Norman keep, built probably, like the White

Tower of London, by a monk of Bec after the Conquest. Then only about six weeks after that I was staying near Colchester and found myself inside the enormous keep of Colchester Castle. By this time I was really getting on the track of the subject. So when a week later I came through a village called Castle Heddingham where there are the remains of a castle with a very well-preserved Norman keep, I took it quite for granted that you enter a Norman keep at first floor level. That was part of the system – if you were under attack it made it much more difficult for the enemy if, instead of bashing in the door at ground level, they had first to get up to the next floor in order to find a way in. These places were built for defence, with huge walls twelve to fifteen feet (sorry, four to five metres) thick. And this is the great attraction of Norman architecture, whether domestic or ecclesiastical, the tremendous sense of solidity, of rock-like sureness. It makes you think of Luther's great hymn:

> *A mighty fortress is our God,*
> *A bulwark never failing;*
> *Our helper he, amid the flood*
> *Of mortal ills prevailing.*

Not, of course, that it is a perfect comparison because eventually people found the way to crack those ancient fortresses and they were no longer the sure defence that they had been.

Whereas we believe of God that he is an everlasting rock, an unendingly safe refuge, a mighty fortress, our saviour and an enduring protection against every ill. This is what the disciples of Jesus were learning all the time they were with him. If you were "with Jesus" it was all right.

2. Rome

This is the story of my lost sock. I was staying in an ancient monastery in Rome built inside a temple, where they had just installed a lot of modern plumbing – had taken, you might say, a great leap into the twentieth century. After the evening meal, with various dripdry items of clothing to be washed, I started to do my laundry in the wash basin in my room. I had reached the stage of washing my socks when to my horror one of them took a sudden dive down the plug hole and disappeared. I should explain that there was no plug in the basin (I learnt my lesson, incidentally, and now always travel with one of those universal plugs). But more than that, this particular type of basin didn't have the sort of metal cross which effectively stops the cap of one's toothpaste or anything else exiting from the basin. "Oh, Lord," I said to myself, "now I shall have to try to get that thing [the U-bend] off from under the basin." But when I got down there was no U-bend and the horrible truth dawned – my sock had gone into the system. Feeling thoroughly disgraced I reported the fact (there was no point in concealing it because all the basins on that corridor very rapidly became blocked). Every imaginable expedient was tried – enough caustic soda was poured down to rot all the sewers of Rome, but no matter how much huffing and puffing went on nothing materialized except odd bits of slime which floated up whenever, throughout the night, I heard a gurgling sound and leaped from my bed to see if it had finally worked; but always in vain. So on the next day an expert with an electrical gadget was brought in, the system was cleared, and I said goodbye to my sock.

But things never happen one at a time – I went to the lavatory and, I could hardly believe it, the chain came away in my hand. I managed to fix that, but every time during the rest of my visit when I pulled it it came away again.

Yes, Lord, I Believe

If that were all! I had just finished having a shower, had dried myself and bent down to put on my sandals, resting my hand lightly, but ever so lightly, on a wash basin (no, not *the* wash basin, this was another one) at the side of the shower, when there was a horrible crunching sound and the wash basin came away from the wall. I have confessed enough and I will draw a veil over the rest of that unfortunate visit and say *Arrivaderci Roma*!

I wish I could tell you that like the woman in the parable who found her lost coin and was able to call friends and neighbours and say, "Come and rejoice with me for I have found the coin that was lost"; or like the shepherd who, when he had recaptured sheep No. 100, was able to gather the rest of the village and say, "I've found it" – I wish I could say the same. Alas, I cannot, my sock is lost for ever in the sewers of that great city.

But I think my story has an even nicer ending. As you know, one travels light nowadays, dripdry nylon and all that, and the loss of one sock of a pair (which renders sock two relatively useless) was disastrous. The way the story ends is with one of the monks coming to me and saying, "Poor you! I hear you've lost one of your socks. Here are two pairs. I don't need them, you have them." Because that is in the Gospel too, isn't it: Love your neighbour as you love yourself.

3. New Orleans

I had been sent by my abbot to visit a monastery in the United States and found myself in Louisiana. Since I grew up in the great days of jazz I expressed a desire to visit New Orleans, and my hosts very kindly took me the two hundred or so miles there by car. When the brother had parked with some difficulty in a little street in the centre of the city, he said he thought there was something the matter with the car and that it wasn't going to start again, the engine being completely lifeless – though how the battery could be flat after driving two hundred miles we couldn't understand. "Well, let's leave it for a while – perhaps it is over-heated", we said, and off we went to see the sights of the city: the Mississippi River (where we saw a steamboat), the cathedral and so on. To my great joy there was even a jazz band playing in the square in front of the cathedral!

But when we got back to the car it was as dead as could be – "Well, let's wait a bit more." It was a very hot day so we went into a nearby ice-cream parlour and had a beautiful ice-cream, and when we came to pay the kind young owner refused to take any money (the second nice memory of New Orleans!). Back to the car, but NO GO.

So the brother rather naïvely said he would go round the corner to the large church and see whether the priest could help. He came back with a very long face, having had the complete brush-off: the priest wouldn't even let him use the phone to contact a garage. What should we do? "Well, we could go back and ask that nice chap in the ice-cream parlour if he can help." So we did, and this time his pretty young wife had arrived. She first apologized for the way she was dressed – which she didn't seem to think suitable when talking to priests – and then said, "Oh, I'll help you!"

She simply went out into the street and hailed the first car, which stopped immediately (the driver obviously thought she was on the game – it was that sort of district). "My friends are in trouble", she said. Out he got, opened up our bonnet, got out his jump leads and proceeded to get us going. It was a very narrow street and a long queue of cars at once started to form behind him, but our friend went all along the row of honking drivers impatient at the hold-up, explaining that "her friends" were in trouble. The car started, she blew us a kiss and off we went.

And I thought: It's the Gospel all over again – no change in the Temple and a good neighbour in the street. So I learnt a lesson and it was quite my happiest memory of the

U.S.A. When I got back to England I wrote a letter to say thank you, carefully addressing it to the Ice Cream Parlour, next to the Louisiana Folk Museum, St Peter's Street – unhappily it came back to me from the U.S. postal authorities marked "Address Unknown". I was sorry about that.

4. Rome Again

When I was young I was an inveterate sightseer, and wherever I went made a point of seeing everything there was to be seen. Now my technique tends to be to limit my seeing to one thing and to look at that carefully, avoiding the indigestion that comes from a surfeit of churches and galleries. The last time I was in Florence I genned up on one church (Santa Maria Novella) and spent about three hours in it and that was that; then I felt free just to sit outside a café with a cappuccino coffee and watch the wonderful world go by.

Mind you, I have an antipathy to the remains of ancient walls. When you get a stump of wall two feet high tracing rather vaguely the foundations of a building, I find that it looks pretty much the same whether it is on the top of Masada or in ancient Ephesus. But I did once spend a concentrated period in the Roman Forum with a first class map and guide book in my hand. It too did in the end defeat me and I retired exhausted. But the point of my telling you this is that as I was slowly moving around two American ladies came up to me (such dears, but archetypal tourists) and asked whether something which (I think) was the Temple of the Vestal Virgins was the spot where Julius Caesar was assassinated. Well, with the aid of my guide book I took them to the correct spot, and then to my astonishment one of them with a voice of wonder said, "Gee, isn't it marvellous to think that's where he said, To be or not to be!"

Wasn't it Dr Routh who said, "Gentlemen, verify your references!" But, you know, we often fail to verify our references. It is very easy to make the unguarded remark, slightly exaggerated perhaps, and then afterwards to realize that what we have said wasn't strictly accurate, wasn't in fact true at all. And then we are in the embarrassing position of not knowing whether to make a point of correcting what we had incorrectly said, with people thinking, "What a lot of fuss about nothing", or whether to leave a false impression, with the niggling feeling that we have been less than truthful. Incidentally, if you cast your mind to holiday tours you have been on, can you remember the valiant attempts to appear interested when you were bored stiff and wished to goodness the guide wouldn't go on so (because you didn't want to hurt his feelings), when all you really wanted was to sit down and rest your feet? How truthful/untruthful ought one to be? It's the old teaser, isn't it: if a lady says to a gentleman, "Do you like my dress?" and he thinks it is ghastly, does a gentleman tell the truth?

Perhaps we need certain façades in order to keep the wheels of society turning smoothly – and that is a mixed metaphor if ever there was one. Perhaps all I'm saying is that life isn't always simple. And perhaps the totally honest person would be very uncomfortable to live with!

14.

Three Good Things in Life

1. Sunshine

Attitudes to things like sun and rain and snow depend very much on whereabouts in the world you live. In a parched land people wait urgently, despairingly, for the rains to come, and those who live in grey northern climes dream of the sun and Spanish beaches. I remember an Italian friend visiting us some years ago who saw what he thought was the moon shining vaguely in the midday sky and was astonished to be told that it was the English sun. For me the sun, as it gets stronger and stronger as winter recedes into the distance, comes as a lovely, warming, encouraging, beaming thing. To take off your clothes and allow the sun's warmth to glow on you, that is the winter dream of Britons by the thousand and the explanation of those curious white bodies that stand out so ashamedly among the deep bronze of the regulars on the beaches of the Mediterranean.

The sun brightens the whole scene and brings a gladness with it. It brings with it a sense of security; it restores life and draws out from nature huge reserves of vitality.

And the sun has always had something of a sense of the divine about it. The famous heretic pharaoh of Egypt, Akhenaton, uncle of Tutankhamen and husband of the lady Nefertiti (who some think the most beautiful woman in the world), was the sponsor of the Sun cult in ancient Egypt – the *worship* of the Sun.

But in biblical tradition too the sun has been a symbol of the hidden Godhead: the Lord God is a sun and a shield, the Sun of Righteousness. Francis of Assisi, we are told in *The Mirror of Perfection*,

> **above all other creatures wanting reason, loved the sun and fire with most affection. For he was wont to say, "In the morning when the sun rises, every man ought to praise God, who created it for our use, because through it our eyes are enlightened by day. Then in the evening when it becomes night, every man ought to give praise on account of Brother Fire, by which our eyes are enlightened by night; for we be all as it were blind, and Our Lord by these two, our brothers, doth enlighten our eyes. And therefore we ought specially to praise the Creator himself for these and other creatures which we daily use." The which he himself did to the day of his death. And because he said and deemed that the sun is fairer than other created things, and is more often likened to our Lord, and that the Lord himself in the scriptures is called the Sun of Righteousness, therefore giving that name to those Praises which he had made of the creatures of the Lord, what time the Lord did certify him of his kingdom, he called them, "The Song of Brother Sun".**

Contemplation of the sun and its brilliance leads us to God who created it: "It was he who made the great lights, for his mercy endures for ever" (Psalm 135). Except not really for ever, for in the great vision at the end of the Book of Revelation, "the city has no need of sun or moon to shine upon it, for the glory of God is its light . . . and there shall be no night there" (21:23, 25).

When I next feel the sun's heat I shall think of that – you too perhaps, as you lie on one of those famous beaches.

2. Sleep

I think if I had to list in order of delight the bodily functions
that I value most, pretty high on the list would come Sleep.
I am one of those lucky ones who in general (though there
are off nights, of course) can put my head on the pillow and
within half a minute be sound asleep. I'm not so successful
at actually staying asleep, and tend to wake up at about
four o'clock only to find that I can't get back to sleep for
an hour or so; and then (what else could you expect?) when
I've really sunk back into a deep slumber it is 5.30 and time
to stir in order to rise for Matins. But when I'm really tired
and I get a really good, restoring night's sleep, then I feel
the full force of that lovely phrase in the psalms "for so he
giveth his beloved sleep" – in other words, what a grace
from God!

I've got on my desk one of those marvellous products of
man's patience and scholarship: a biblical concordance
which in alphabetical order lists, reference by reference,
the words of the Bible. Mine is Robert Young's *Analytical
Concordance of the Holy Bible, Eighth Edition, thoroughly
revised*. It describes itself as "containing about 311,000
references". Imagine it! And from the days before
computers! What sleepless nights for poor Robert Young!
It is further "subdivided under the Hebrew and Greek
originals with the literal meaning and pronunciation of
each; also index lexicons to the Old and New Testaments,
being a guide to parallel passages". It is a compilation
whose making required, I think, a high degree of
perseverance and a special kind of mind. One of the most
famous makers of concordances, Alexander Cruden, did in
fact go mad.

But what a joy to have and use! To take, for instance,
a word like SLEEP, to see how it is used and where it is
used in the Bible, and to find – and this is the way whenever

one starts looking up words in dictionaries or articles in encyclopedias – that one is led up all sorts of unexpected vistas.

"SLEEP", Genesis 2:21: "He caused a deep sleep to fall upon Adam and he slept." You remember, it is the story of the creation of the world and of man, and while Adam sleeps, out of his side God takes a rib and creates Eve. And that, you see, makes me think immediately (truly!) of an ancient sermon preached to the newly baptized by St John Chrysostom in Constantinople on Easter Day 1600 years ago. St John sees Christ's dead body on the cross, "sleeping" in death, and out of his side comes blood and water (the symbols of Baptism and the Eucharist, symbols of the Church), and the preacher sees a new Eve, the Church, being born from the pierced side of the sleeping New Adam.

And there is another thought, "God is never sleeping". My concordance gives me the lead: Psalm 44, verse 23, where the psalmist reproaches a God who appears to have gone to sleep: "Up, Lord, why sleepest thou; awake and be not absent from us for ever; wherefore hidest thou thy face and forgettest our misery and trouble?" But because God is in fact never asleep we can sleep in safety, secure under his protection: "I laid me down and slept, and rose again; for the Lord has sustained me . . . I will lay me down in peace and take my rest; for it is thou, Lord, only that makest me dwell in safety . . . he will not suffer thy foot to be moved, and he that keepeth thee will not sleep – Behold, he that keepeth Israel shall neither slumber nor sleep. The Lord himself is thy keeper; the Lord is thy defence upon thy right hand . . ."

There are 136 references to "sleep" in my concordance. But my favourite one is "he giveth his beloved sleep".

3. Food

I wonder if you would be able to pick out the most
memorable meal you have ever had in your life? If we put
together the most memorable meals of everybody reading
this and combined all the suggestions we would end up, no
doubt, with an absolutely gargantuan banquet. I like trying
out different foods when I am away from home, so my
memories stretch from good old roast beef and all that, via
spaghetti Bolognese to homous and Tandoori chicken.
And that covers more than a half century of eating, from
bread and milk as a baby to good red steaks. Yet if I had
to say which was the one meal which has, over all these
years, remained most in my memory, the one of which I can
still recall the deliciousness of its taste (and I can say this
without offending anyone who may have cooked me what
would be truly a "triumph of the culinary art") dates from
a bitterly cold day during the war when we were stationed,
wet and miserable, somewhere in the uplands behind
Cassino. Very cold and hungry I bought from some
villagers a handful of apples. They were small with very
mottled skins and would most certainly not conform to
EEC requirements as to size and quality. But how I can still
recall those delicious apples!

They were food, lovely food, for a cold and empty
stomach. Though I have eaten (even over-eaten) and
enjoyed many a meal cooked with beautiful sauces, it is
those apples that stand out in my memory, and what made
them so memorable was the sharpness of my appetite.

Now the same thing operates in the realm of the spirit.
If you are really hungry, you really do appreciate having
something to eat. And if you have a spiritual hunger, if you
have a spiritual appetite, you will appreciate spiritual food.
I mean, had I been offered those apples after just walking
out of the best restaurant in Naples (whatever that may be

– I've never been in it), I'm sure I wouldn't have looked at them twice. If I were regularly glutting my appetite, the edge of appreciation would be dulled. It's a bit like the time I gave up smoking (after multiple failures, I hasten to add, lest you think I am a man of strong will power), and the capacity to taste and to smell things returned. If we appreciate the sheer goodness of food – the way it can restore our bodily powers, that glow of well-being when our body has been properly fed – we can better understand what is waiting for us when we come with sharpened appetites, uncoarsened appetites, to the things of the spirit.

The Bible talks about life with God, our sharing in the life of the Godhead, the life of the Spirit, precisely in these terms of eating and drinking: Bread of Life, Cup of Salvation, Heavenly Banquet, Marriage Feast, Lord's Supper . . .

And in the prayer which Jesus gave to his disciples as a very pattern for all prayer, Christians have always understood that in that phrase, "Give us this day our daily bread", there is a double sense. We need to eat our dinner, Lord, but also: feed us with bread from heaven, food for the spirit.

15. *Three Words*

1. Death

When I was a boy I used to irritate a favourite aunt of mine intensely by singing what must have been a popular song of the time (I remember we had it on a gramophone record), "Ain't It Grand to be Bloomin' Well Dead?" She thought it highly irreverent and not at all "nice". And though I don't sing it now (indeed, I can't remember any more of the words), it had a robustness about it which seems to me rather more healthy than the current attitude to death which has made it the great taboo subject of modern society. Once upon a time it was sex that was the forbidden topic, swept under the carpet, and all the really bad swear words were sexual ones. Now sex swear words are commonplace and pretty meaningless – their ultra-frequency merely betokening a very limited vocabulary. But it is death (or perhaps not so much death as dying) that we don't want to talk about, and we wait for "cancer" or "ashes" to become bad swear words. So we shut death away in geriatric wards; we don't want people to be told that they are dying, though they may well know it better than we do ourselves and keep up the pretence for our benefit. We try to anaesthetize the whole subject.

But it is the one thing that won't go away, the one absolutely irreversible and inevitable fact of life.

How very different from the attitude of mediaeval man, who had great paintings on the walls of his churches of the Dance of Death, permanent reminders to kings and popes as well as to ordinary folk of their ultimate destiny. There used indeed, until quite recent times, at the coronations of popes (including the Borgias!) to be a ceremony when in the midst of all the pomp a burning flax was extinguished in front of the man sitting there in all his glory and he was told, "*Beatissime Pater, sic transit gloria mundi*" – thus the glory of the world passes.

However, it was not just mediaeval man, not just Christian society, which was aware of the reality of death, of the need to come to terms with it. Archaeology has amply demonstrated, whether in Egypt or in recent excavations in China, that other civilizations coped with the fact of death in a way that ours today seems incapable of. "Men fear death as children fear to go into the dark", wrote Francis Bacon. Because today for so many people death means darkness it has become a horror, and a suitable subject for video nasties.

But death is only a horizon, and the point about horizons is that they don't in fact exist, they are simply "as far as the eye can see". If there is a beyond-death then things look very different. If all that is here survives, indeed not merely survives but is able to come to a new flowering, why should we be afraid to encounter it in others or in ourselves? Of course there is a sense of loss, but for St Paul "death is swallowed up in victory".

So it isn't, or shouldn't, be a morbid subject. Francis of Assisi called it Sister Death. The really schizophrenic attitude is to behave as though it will never happen.

2. Parish

If you think about it, we do take an awful lot of words for granted. How many times does a man say, for example, "My wife", and how many would know that if you looked it up in the dictionary you would find that its derivation is "Old English: WIF; Old Saxon: WIF; Old High German: WIP; Old Norse: VIF; Ultimate Origin: UNKNOWN"? The other way round is easier, but I bet most women who say "My husband" would be hard put to it to expound the word: "Old English: HUSBONDA from Old Norse:

HÚSBÓNDI; see House and Bond." Well, we won't go on about that, because the only point I'm really making is that we do use words without thinking about them.

You may make use of the daily notes of the Bible Reading Fellowship (there are hundreds of thousands of users throughout the world), and I recently came across a comment in one of their notes on 1 Peter 2:11, "Beloved, as sojourners and exiles I appeal to you":

> **Peter here uses an unusually interesting word,**
> ***Paroiki***, **a word meaning sojourners or people**
> **away from home. Primarily used of Jews dispersed**
> **throughout the Roman empire, he uses it here of**
> **Christians. They were not at home, they were born**
> **into a new nation, temporary visitors whose real**
> **home was in heaven. [Now here comes the**
> **punchline:] About six centuries later when**
> **Theodore came to Canterbury as archbishop, he**
> **divided England into parochiae, parishes. We see**
> **at once the link with Peter's word. Theodore's idea**
> **was that Christians were colonies of heaven –**
> **outposts in a pagan country, which was exactly**
> **Peter's idea.**

That also is something interesting: "when Theodore came to Canterbury as archbishop", because do you know where he came from? He was an Asiatic Greek, educated at Tarsus and Athens, and he ended up as archbishop in England! That was in the seventh century – and we love to talk nowadays of one world as though the idea were new!

I remember once looking in the archives of our monastery in Tuscany to see where, in the fourteenth century, the monks had come from who were to end up in a totally isolated monastery in the depths of the Tuscan countryside. Well, they came from everywhere: from Spain, from Poland, from Germany, from the Low Countries, from

France and at least two from England. The Middle Ages may have been very local-city-or-province-conscious, but they were surely also internationally minded.

Anyway, to get back to the point, here's me, who had been a parish priest for twenty-seven years – and having used the word "parish" goodness knows how many times during that period – suddenly pulled up short by this commentary on what the word is actually derived from. It isn't a place where people settle, stay put, put down roots and get all cosy together – it's a place where people are just "visitors" and are "on the move"! How much of parish strategy is based on the opposite assumption!

Mind you, it isn't in fact certain that it was Theodore who introduced the parish system to England (there are other theories), but it is the word itself which is so interesting. When you read the description of the martyrdom of St Polycarp, which took place at Smyrna (now Izmir) in the second century, written by the Christians of Smyrna and sent out as a sort of circular letter to put the other Christian communities in the picture, you find they entitle it "The Church of God of the Parish of Smyrna to the Church of God of the Parish in Philomelium", but what in Greek they are actually saying is "From the Church of God who are temporary visitors in Smyrna to the temporary visiting Church of God in Philomelium". When we say someone is very parochially minded, meaning very tied down to his little patch, very narrow, locally minded, we are in fact turning the language of the New Testament upside down. A real "parishioner" sees much more largely than that, more like John Wesley with his "Wide world my parish", though even that is a little bit "parochial".

3. *Logos and* Logos

You must, almost certainly, have sat in a crowded bus or tube and, having read all the advertisements, seen something in a newspaper two seats away which caught your eye, and then found that the wretched man reading it always managed to hold and turn it in such a way that you simply couldn't finish reading the headline: VOTE OF CONFIDENCE GOVERNMENT . . . was it FALLS or WINS?

I find the same thing with the badges people wear as I struggle to decipher them. I can identify ROTARY at a glance, and LONDON TRANSPORT, and can make a fair guess at one or other Trade Union badges. But now there is this fantastic variety of multi-coloured badges – ELVIS, THE WHO and goodness knows what else.

When I was going up to the BBC one day to record a "Thought for the Day", there in the tube three seats away was a young chap wearing one with writing so small that it took me ages to get the hang of it. I got it more or less a word at a time as he moved about in his seat, bent forward to pick up his book and so on. But one has to be discreet and I only just managed to finish the message before he got out at his station. Having read the message I was left struggling to *get* the message, because what it said was quite simply: THE FUTURE IS FEMALE. Did it mean that his future depended on the girl he was going to marry? Was it some kind of public Valentine card (not really, since it was December)? Was he a male supporter of women's lib? Was it a philosophical statement about the past and the present giving birth to what is still to come? Was it affirming the end of a male-dominated society? I still haven't discovered. It was rather like one of those bits of conversation one overhears as a couple go past, which come without beginning or end and leave one's imagination working overtime.

There is now the frequent addition to certain posters of the simple statement: THIS DEGRADES WOMEN, and I must say that I think they are right. There was the graffito I saw in Camden Town which said: LOUISE IS A TEST

TUBE BABY – meant presumably as a deadly insult, but who knows? It is all part of an attempt to communicate in a society which doesn't make communication, real communication, easy. I suppose it is the same urge that makes people say their thing in the anonymity of phone-in programmes. A lot of people find words hard to put flesh to – and that is a pity because words are rather special.

"GOD SAID" is one of the most marvellous phrases in the Bible. God said and it was done. God spoke a word, a *LOGOS*, and his Word became flesh – so potent and so active a Word that it was enfleshed and dwelt among us. And that WORD INCARNATE, the *LOGOS*, has echoed down the centuries, powerful and active, communicating life, the Word of God who is Jesus the Christ.

One of the great advantages of being made to learn things by rote as a child – poems, psalms, collects – is that bits and phrases come back again years later. I can still sing in Greek years later a translation of "Oh, dear, what can the matter be", learnt as a boy. I can still recall the Book of Common Prayer collect for the fourth Sunday of Advent: "O Lord, raise up, we pray thee, thy power and come among us, and with great might succour us."

One phrase which I treasure I found on a memorial card given to me a few years ago – something by Edith Sitwell. I couldn't say how many times it has re-echoed for me. I would love to wear it as a badge for people to peer at and decipher in the tube, but I give it to you as a thought, hoping that it may be as powerful for you as it has been for me:

LOVE IS NOT CHANGED BY DEATH AND NOTHING IS LOST. ALL IN THE END IS HARVEST.

16. *On Being Ordinary*

1. The Empty Pumps

During a great petrol shortage not long ago, in pubs and at parties up and down the country people were telling boring stories about how, when they were within three cars of the petrol pump, it ran dry, or how they managed to get a few gallons at a little garage round the corner. Let me bore you with mine.

What happened was that I waited until my tank was two-thirds empty in order not to aggravate the queuing situation (very public-spirited and all that!), and then when I got to my regular garage, it being pointless to go to the other one which was serving "regular customers only", I found a huge notice which said PRE-PAID ACCOUNTS AND DOCTORS ETC. ONLY. So I walked into the forecourt (I hadn't driven there, in order not to waste the precious liquid) and asked "meekly" whether clergy counted among the etceteras.

I was then passed from petrol pump assistant to petrol pump assistant (each one professing not to know the answer), until I was face to face with the manager, who said, "Well, no, clergymen are not etceteras." In fairness I should add that he did eventually relent and, telling me that they would be shut for the next week, allowed me to be filled up with three gallons. But it did start me thinking. Obviously the days are long past when the clergy were treated as part of a socially superior class. Equally obviously one Roman Catholic priest in a North London suburb hasn't the same clout as the priest back in Ireland whom a parishioner once told me about. The Canon used to go round the hedgerows of his parish in the evening with his hawthorn stick to rout out the courting couples – and he got away with it! That's interesting too, because the person telling me this spoke of him not just with awe but with affection – a certain eccentricity in priests and headmasters is tolerated.

Anyway, as I say, the modern suburban clergy can't lay claim to anything very upmarket, but not even to be behind doctors as an "etcetera" did seem a rather drastic writing off of one's sociological usefulness.

But then several days later, having celebrated Christmas and Bethlehem and the stable and all that, it suddenly occurred to me that, had it been a question of refuelling donkeys a certain family – though it was engaged on the most important journey ever: the Eternal Word of God arriving on the earthly scene – would also have been an "etcetera". So what was I worrying about! As St Paul reminded the Corinthians, we really are very small fry: "Not many of you were wise according to worldly standards, not many were powerful, not many were of noble birth" (1 Corinthians 1:26). If you ever go to Capernaum you will see that they have in recent years excavated what was, with high probability, the remains of the house of St Peter, and it is the most grotty one-room hovel, in a block of grotty one-room hovels, you can imagine. It is good to be reminded from time to time of our origins, our real status, which one so easily forgot in the petrol pump queue.

It would be a funny old world if we did always remember it, except that it would be a funny NEW world, the world of the new creation, the world that began at Bethlehem.

2. Buck House

London in the summer is the season for Royal Garden Parties, when the privileged few make their way through those gates so ceremoniously guarded by troops detailed for the defence of the Sovereign, whilst outside, pressed against the railings, stand the envious onlookers who would dearly love to get in behind the scenes.

Well, I will let you into a kind of secret, in that not many people know about it. Unless the clampdown on security has now changed things, if you are over fourteen years of age, the next time you turn up at Buckingham Palace, all you need to do is go up to the policeman on duty and say that you want to sign the visitors' book. You are then wafted across the great courtyard, to the astonishment and envy of all the people around, and ushered into a small room where lies Her Majesty's Visitors' Book. I've no idea who looks at it afterwards – I'm sure the Queen doesn't – but at least you have got inside Buck House!

Of course, if you want to see the real thing you can always go to one of the other royal residences, such as Windsor Castle, and though there are places where you are not allowed to go, you will see more of royal state than you are able to get a glimpse of in the room housing the visitors' book in Buckingham Palace.

I would guess that for a lot of us our picture of heaven is a bit like that. Since we have never got past the gates all we can do is fantasize about what it is like inside, and fed as we are on visions of glorious thrones and precious stones and golden crowns and trumpets and the rest, we fairly easily think of heaven in terms of Buckingham Palace, the Vatican, the Louvre Museum and Westminster Abbey all rolled into one, with a massed choir and orchestra to outshine all others.

But since most of us don't come from that sort of milieu, since most of us don't live in stately homes, isn't that rather an unfortunate image to be landed with? If heaven is coming to the Father, to our Father, in perfect joy, if I live, say, in a council house in London, wouldn't a better image be coming home into the back garden to find the family sitting on the grass?

Mind you, heaven may very well be nicer than where you

live now. I'm sure the writer of the hymn "Jerusalem, my happy home" felt very strongly that way as he wrote of his picture-heaven:

> *Thy walls are made of precious stones,*
>   *Thy bulwarks diamonds square;*
> *Thy gates are of right orient pearl;*
>   *Exceeding rich and rare;*
>
> *Thy houses are of ivory,*
>   *Thy windows crystal clear;*
> *Thy tiles are made of beaten gold –*
>   *O God, that I were there!*

But I sense envy in his next verse:

> *Within thy gates no thing doth come*
>   *That is not passing clean,*
> *No spider's web, no dirt, no dust,*
>   *No filth may there be seen.*

That is, I suspect a man who had problems about keeping his place clean and who was thoroughly fed up with constant dusting.

But just as it isn't a wall-to-wall carpet that makes a house a home, so surely it isn't the vision of jewelled walls that makes heaven. It is the presence of the Father and his family. It is truly coming home. It is the warmth of love. It isn't getting lost among vast multitudes or down unending vistas.

After all, you wouldn't really want to *live* in Buckingham Palace, would you?

17. *Society*

"I saw nothing but violence and strife in the city" – a newspaper report from New York? The latest news from the Lebanon? Evidence at an inquiry into one of our inner-city areas? It could well be, but it is in fact a verse of the fifty-fourth psalm (or Psalm 55, according to the way you number them), from way, way back, from ancient Israel. So although we may think that violence and terror is a mark of our age, as our newspapers and television screens fill up with muggings and rapes and murders, it is an old, old story. I very much doubt that London in the eighteenth century was a safer place to live in than the London of the 1980s, in fact I'm sure it wasn't. If I read Runciman's *History of the Crusades*, with all the pillage and rape and bloodbaths that so often accompanied them, or if I recall the systematic torture – rack, thumbscrews, hanging, drawing and quarterings – that went on for centuries, I wonder if our age is engaged in anything very new. There may be new techniques, but it is still violence and strife.

Perhaps it is that today we are more highly strung and that we shudder more easily? I remember once going round Nelson's flagship, *Victory*, and being shown the conditions in which men's legs were amputated below decks during battles – when their stumps were dipped into buckets of pitch to cauterize them – and the very thought of it makes one shiver.

But there is more to it than that. Whenever life is devalued all sorts of things, horrible things, become possible. When sex is devalued, becomes just another "thing", rape becomes just another way to treat a body.

What I find difficult to understand is "idealistic" terror – terror engaged in for the sake of an ideal. I once quite by chance and some years ago (and in another country) found myself invited to a flat which turned out to be the operational HQ of a hi-jack. The leader was already in jail, but his wife and friends were there, and what struck me was that they were perfectly ordinary, I would say even gentle, people. I am baffled when I try to penetrate their mind.

Is it perhaps that we are horrified to find that what we thought were our high modern moral standards (the idea that society has risen way above the Dark Ages), our optimistic assessments, are misplaced? Is it perhaps that we still have deep within each one of us violent, rapist tendencies in our dark recesses?

The psalmist's reaction was, "O that I had wings like a dove to fly away and be at rest. So I would escape far away and take refuge in the desert. I would hasten to find a shelter from the raging wind, from the destructive storm, O Lord, and from their plotting tongues." But we have no desert to fly to. And the enemy is all too often hidden in our own hearts: "Each evening they come back like dogs. They howl and roam about the city, they prowl in search of food, they snarl till they have their fill" (Psalm 58). In the end the constant message of the psalmist is that we have no alternative but to put our trust in God. "O Lord, it is you who are my strength, it is you to whom I turn, for you, O God, are my stronghold" – small consolation, you may think, if you have just been mugged. But if God is left out of the picture where, oh where, do we end up?

I was talking to someone the other day, a family man and a Christian, whose son has joined up with one of the cult religions from the East, one of many young people who have taken refuge in such groups. It is part of a contemporary attempt to "fly away . . . to take refuge in the desert".

Well, I don't doubt that there is a lot of humbug and that there are some very disturbing features attached to some of these cults. I realize also that quite a lot of people having drifted into them drift out (the Beatles, you will recall, were into the Eastern cult scene at one stage), but the popularity of the cults certainly highlights the failure of the Christian Churches to offer, especially to the young, any real spiritual experience – above all, I think, any real experience of prayer. I once did a series of Sunday evening broadcasts on prayer, and at the end said, "If you want to take this up there are vicarages and presbyteries and convents all over the country, go and knock at the door and ask for help", and someone wrote to me and said, "You must be joking!"

I have no illusions. I don't for a moment imagine that all over the country, in discotheques and youth clubs, there are hundreds of people looking for a spiritual dimension to life, searching and seeking. But seeing that these cults prosper, that people make the trek to India, does highlight the fact that there is a spiritual vacuum and that the Churches have failed to fill it, have failed to satisfy the hunger for a spiritual experience which is for real.

One answer is for the Churches to involve themselves heavily in social concerns, and thank God that is happening more and more. There is no doubt that a lot of young people respond very readily to such demands, often very heavy demands, on their goodness in order to help those in need. Thank God, the Churches are increasingly aware of their role in defending the rights of the needy – the Gospel as it is proclaimed in South America has a bite and relevance in it which has all too often been lacking. But it is not the heart of the message they have to deliver, even though it is an essential test of the reality of the Gospel and their commitment to it. If the Church does not show the way into a real personal relationship with the ultimate mystery, if the Church is nothing more than a welfare organization, then the Church fails in its essential mission, and people who are seekers inevitably look elsewhere.

Yet we can't say "the Church" and just shift the

responsibility onto some vague "them". It is *us* – and if our lives are not real, if we are not into the mystery, how in heaven's name do we answer them? What is quite ridiculous is that there is an enormous treasure in Christian tradition waiting to be tapped. Jesus offered "living waters": why then should people be satisfied with empty cisterns?

One of the more encouraging aspects of our contemporary society is surely DIY, Do It Yourself. No doubt we are driven to it in the first place by rising costs. Get an estimate for someone to come and decorate your sitting room and you get a shock. So instead you decide to do it yourself and have a go. There are probably a few first failures – the wretched paper, all covered in goo, falls away from the wall where you have so laboriously placed it and drapes itself over your head – but then you discover the thrill of having finally succeeded and you stand back and have a marvellous sense of having DONE SOMETHING. Well, maybe it doesn't join absolutely perfectly, but on the whole . . .

We are not meant to be helpless creatures, we are all artists. "An artist is not a special kind of man, everyone is a special kind of artist" (Eric Gill). We are a talented people, and when people use their talents they become more fully human. So I think we must give ourselves, in this modern society of ours, a plus mark as more and more people learn to be truly themselves, to realize their potential, which means theologically, to be more human, more like what God made us to be. There was once an old lady who went to see Shakespeare's *Hamlet* and when asked what she thought of it, said, "Not much, it was just a lot of quotations!" You may recall one of those quotes: "What a piece of work is man! how noble in reason! how infinite in faculty! in form, in moving, how express and admirable! in action how like an angel! in apprehension how like a god! the beauty of the world! the paragon of animals!"

Man made in the image of God, in the image of the Creator – Man the Creator, called to share in the divine activity and called to enrich the world with his talents!

Called too to respect the things of creation – to respect the nature of nails and saws. I love that piece in Eric Gill's autobiography where he tells how he was taught that there was a right and a wrong way to sharpen a pencil – you can hack it in a way which is disrespectful of the nature of a pencil, or you can sharpen it in a way which respects it and which is something beautiful. The more we "do it ourselves", the more we begin to understand the nature of things, and then the way we "do" is part of the way we "are" and our activity becomes a prayer. There is an old Latin tag *Laborare est orare* – to work is to pray – which is sometimes misused to make work a substitute for prayer, which it cannot be; doing and making is not a substitute but it is a part of prayer. A well-hung wallpaper becomes an act of worship. That doesn't mean that next Sunday morning one says, "Well, instead of going to church I'll redecorate the bedroom", but it could mean that your prayer will be all the richer because you have also decorated the bedroom. Will it sound trite and too banal for words if I say that Jesus was a carpenter? – if ever doing and being were one in a man, surely it was in him. So good luck, when you finally get round to tackling the kitchen!

If we get a plus mark for DIY, there is another side of life today which I think gets a minus, or at least a very poor pass, and that is the way we seek to escape from reality.

I suppose one of the biggest growth industries at present must be the video tape or disc, with video shops sprouting in every High Street and Shopping Centre. So if the long hours in front of the TV have begun to pall, there is now a new escape mechanism, the video. One more escape route to add to the discotheque and all the others. The trouble is that it is passive. The great advantage of radio over TV (or for that matter, the advantage of a good book) is that it gives

Society

scope for the imagination, whereas the box and the video leave very little to the imagination, or even nothing at all (and I am not referring to full frontal exposure).

There is going to be an awful lot of leisure time for a lot of us in the future, if not through the continuing curse of unemployment, then through technological advances. I was told the other day of an engineering firm which had, quite typically, reduced its workforce from one thousand to seven hundred in three years, and had now so reorganized itself that there will be no need for them to take on any new staff when business picks up. So is our society to go passively along escape routes?

What are we heading for? And what are we doing to our planet? I would be stupid if I thought that everybody goes round every day worrying about this – we aren't that neurotic!

It is equally true that if some issue bugs us we tend to expect it to bug other people too. For instance, I'm what you might call a religious person by profession and it is easy for me to think that everybody else must be mulling over religious problems. I am well aware that a politician would be horrified by the little amount of time I give to thinking about political issues. But I believe there are an increasing number of people, with or without religious affiliations, who ask themselves, "Where on earth are we going to on earth?" (I might put it in terms of, "Where in heaven's name are we going to on earth?") And at least the nuclear arms issue has made people sit up and think.

We can't opt out of the world. "Stop the world, I want to get off", is a non-starter. And we each of us have some responsibility for what happens. Each of us every day is faced with this responsibility; we may well try to shrug it off, but it won't go away.

Not least we have a prayer responsibility, which means a responsibility to be available before God – to be usable by God, to be a "Here I am" before God.

We have a responsibility to praise God for this world of ours, and to support with our prayer all that men and women are seeking to do and achieve for good. We have a responsibility to intercede for this world of ours, to circle it with prayer, and to hold in prayer those who are in a position to make decisions which determine the course of history. You may love or hate Maggie Thatcher, but either way she needs our prayers. The men in the White House and in the Kremlin, the Ayatollahs – in whose hands the destiny of our earth so very much lies – whether or not they think so, need each day and this day to be "comforted", that is to say "strengthened for good", by your prayers and mine.

18. *Thoughts at the Beginning of a New Year*

January the First. Where will this year take us? I don't want to know. Or do I? No, I think Newman was right: I do not ask to see the distant scene, one step enough for me.

My mind always goes back, on the first day of the year, to a Christmas broadcast of King George VI in 1939, the first year of the Second World War, when he quoted these words: "And I said to the man who stood at the gate of the year: Give me a light, that I may tread safely into the unknown. And he replied: Go out into the darkness, and put your hand into the hand of God. That shall be to you better than light and safer than a known way."

Do I want to know what the year will bring? No, I am content to walk in the dark – what they call "by faith" – because I think it is safer to walk in the dark with him beside me than to lose my way on my own in broad daylight. Don't get me wrong. I don't mean that I'm a bit of a looney, jaywalking down the road, ready to be knocked over by the first of the enormous lorries that now rush past in our narrow streets. I simply mean that we have to co-operate with God and his purposes. But the year belongs (I use the present tense you notice, though 364 days have still to roll by), the year belongs, as does all time, to him, and it is better that way.

There is a passage in St Thomas Aquinas where he says that it is much better to hobble along on the right road than to rush along in the wrong direction. However slowly one goes, at least all the time one is going in the right direction. The one who is running in the wrong direction is getting further and further away from his destination.

And the Way is Christ; if you want to be right, stay close to him! On his progress towards the Celestial City Bunyan's pilgrim made the mistake of leaving the right road when it got rough, and with his companion Hopeful took the path which was "very easy to their feet" and led them to the Castle of Giant Despair. I speak, of course, as a Christian, which you may not be. Transpose it to whatever terms you will: Hold Fast by God!

All around us there is a sense of "instability", even of "fear" – it is one of the signs of our times – a sense that things are lurching uncontrollably, not just in the little patch that each one of us occupies individually, but on the world scale. As tension mounts in this or that part of the world, behind everything there is the spectre of a nuclear war. And though there is no point in working oneself up into a tizzy over something that may never happen, always it is there in the background. I suppose the First World War shattered the Edwardian sense of security, but now the spectre is growing to mammoth proportions, and since Hiroshima a whole generation has grown up that has never known a world where the threat of a tremendous cataclysm has not existed. And it is just not possible to live in such a world without its having an effect on the way people are.

That sort of threat gnaws at our sense of stability. One notices it, for instance, in the way people are reluctant to enter into a binding marriage relationship, the number of people who cohabit rather than take on a life-long commitment. One notices it in the way people are reluctant to commit themselves to take life-vows as monks or nuns, to commit themselves for the rest of their lives. For many people the Future with a capital "F" has acquired a huge question mark, a huge point of interrogation. I don't want to sound off a jeremiad about "materialism", the frenzy of spending on things, but that too is fostered by this same uncertainty: Let us eat, drink and be merry, for tomorrow we die.

Thoughts at the Beginning of a New Year

In one sense the fact that here we have "no abiding city", that "our days pass away like grass", that "man is no more than a breath", has planted a certain pessimism in the Christian tradition. But if it is not kept in balance with the surety that GOD IS, that he is a rock, a stronghold, we end up in a hopelessness which is anything but Christian.

One of London's free entertainments is being able to walk into an auction room. I remember once that some autograph letters were being auctioned (one single letter of Lucrezia Borgia fetched £8500), and all sorts of other interesting or beautiful things were up for auction for a variety of reasons – because the owners needed money, because the owners had died and their assets were being realized for the benefit of others. The auction room is a bit of a Vanity Fair. If you want a living parable of the words of Jesus there you have it. "Fool! This night your soul is required of you; and the things you have prepared, whose will they be?" (Luke 12:20). It isn't even that those with money to buy these treasures will enter into settled possession; the stuff will be back in the auction rooms again one day and the lesson repeated . . . going, going, gone. You can't take it with you – we will all come under the hammer one day.

There is a story of the famous Father Martindale S.J. who was sitting in a railway compartment reading his breviary when a man sitting, disapprovingly, opposite him finally exploded, "Parsons is bloody!" Father Martindale lifted his eyes momentarily to say, "Not so bloody as some." To which the man could only answer, "Well, I'll be damned!", to which Father Martindale sweetly replied, "Not necessarily." Well, I'm a monk and not a parson, and I assume that if you have read this far you do not object to my talking like one. And I would like to suggest, as the monks of old used to say, that we should look at things and at the new year "*sub specie aeternitatis*", from the perspective of eternity, in the light of eternity.

Governments come and go, and I do not wish to belittle their importance, yet in a sense I do belittle them, against the great sweep of the panorama of history and even more against the background of eternity – perspectives do change. And if this is true of great events it is still more true of the mini things that happen. Did the toast burn this morning? Disaster! – not really, "*sub specie aeternitatis*". Have I got a headache? Ghastly, the whole day ruined! Well, not really, "*sub specie aeternitatis*". The trouble is that those of us who believe in eternity often act and talk as though we didn't – on top of the world one moment, down in the dumps the next. We lack a certain "detachment".

And yet once we've got our perspectives right, in a very real sense what happens now *is* all that matters. When someone asked St Charles Borromeo what he would do if, when he were playing a game of chess, he learned that the world would come to an end in five minutes (expecting the answer that he would get down on his knees and pray), the answer he gave was that he would finish the game of chess. "*Sub specie aeternitatis*", if he was right to be doing it at all, there would be nothing wrong if that was what the Lord found him doing when he came.

19. *An Epilogue on Unity*

Unlike the rest of this book this talk was not broadcast but was given at Turvey in the Week of Prayer for Christian Unity in 1984.

I grew up in an era when, at least from the Roman Catholic side, Christian unity was seen essentially in terms of "conversion" (not in the sense of *metanoia* or a new turning to the Lord, but becoming a Roman Catholic), in terms of "re-union".

That is to say, there was the Roman Catholic Church (though many of its members disliked the use of the additional word "Roman" – it was simply and solely the Catholic Church), and the way forward was for heretics and schismatics to renounce the error of their ways and be re-united with THE Church. That Church was seen in extremely monolithic terms, a single solid rock of granite-like dogmas, subject to an unassailable authority, the Pope of Rome, and unvaried and unmoving in its expression. This picture of the Church, though extremely popular, was in fact a caricature both historically and theologically. Historically, it had witnessed many changes over the centuries; the papacy itself had in its actual mode of operation changed and was still changing, and the reality was far less monolithic than was popularly supposed, for instance, in matters liturgical and in schools of spirituality, to mention but two areas.

In fact, already in the 1920s the seeds were sown of much that was to come to fruition with the Second Vatican Council. Some ecumenical worms had begun to creep out of the Roman Catholic woodwork. The famous Conversations at Malines, between Anglican and Roman

Catholic theologians, had taken place, though the end result had been a stiffening of the official Roman attitude and the publication of *Mortalium Animos*, which put a considerable damper on further initiatives. Dom Lambert Beauduin (the author of the paper read at Malines about the Church of England, "United but not absorbed") was exiled from his monastery, and the parallel monastery in Belgium founded to work for Christian Unity by Dom Constantine Bosschaerts had its male section closed. In England the work was quietly developing with men like Father Henry St John O.P. and Dom Bede Winslow O.S.B. of Ramsgate, but it was a work surrounded by immense suspicion. It was through Father Bede (who had founded the review *Eastern Churches Quarterly*) that my horizons were becoming enlarged to realize the importance of the dimension of Eastern Orthodoxy, and the damage which had been done to the West's spirituality by the split with the East.

There was a further enlargement as I became increasingly conscious of my debt to the Anglican tradition in which I had been reared, and the great riches of scriptural and christological devotion which had been fed into me, and also the particular ethos of Anglican worship at its best as I had known it.

By this time Rome was beginning to loosen up – the liturgical reforms of Pius XII had taken place and we were on the threshold of a new era with John XXIII and the Second Vatican Council. Windows were being opened and a new spirit was abroad. The work of Abbé Couturier had begun to bear fruit, and the old Church Unity Octave was transformed into the Week of Prayer for Christian Unity. The Council over, the windows remained open, indeed opened wider, under a pope, Paul VI, whom, I believe, history will recognize as one of the greatest of popes.

For me the horizon was continually widening. I was getting to know various forms of non-conformity – I remember being immensely impressed by the Methodist Covenant Service and, of course, by Wesley's sacramental hymns. I had become a close friend of a Baptist and of a Congregationalist minister and appreciated their particular emphases on the importance of the local *ecclesia*, which adjusts the balance in what would otherwise be an over-centralization, the great *Catholica*, so important in our tradition. The Church Universal, closely bound together, needs that awareness of the local community. From them too I saw anew the importance of the laity as truly a holy priesthood. A Baptist baptism by immersion also left a great impression on me – happily, in the new R.C. rite of baptism that is now officially the first option, though it is not yet a norm.

And Vatican II set its seal on all this with its Decree on Ecumenism, and its recognition of the richness of other traditions and of the fact that these other Churches (or ecclesial bodies, as it chose to call them – Paul VI went further and referred to the Church of England as "our beloved sister Church") had been and were *as such* channels of God's grace. We had travelled a long way! But there was more to come. There were timid initial contacts with Pentecostals – I recall a meeting of a dozen Roman Catholic priests with a leading Pentecostalist who gave us our first experience of praying in tongues. That was quite some time before the Charismatic Renewal hit the Roman scene in the way it has now done, to open up still more windows.

So I was getting to know people and traditions of Christian living and appreciating them as fellow disciples. The Holy Spirit had been at work to transform attitudes in an exhilarating way in so short a period. It is not very long since Eric Abbott, then Dean of Westminster Abbey, held a meeting in the Jerusalem Chamber each year, to which he invited ten Roman Catholics and ten Anglicans simply to meet and chat, and then afterwards to go and pray together in silence for half an hour at the shrine of the Confessor; and I remember a discussion with Patrick O'Donovan when it was decided that it would be more prudent if he did not write about these goings on!

The awareness of the fractured nature of Christ's Church was both partly sharpened (the division and separation at the Holy Table) and partly eased (as one realized that in the one baptism and in devotion to the One Lord there was yet a profound unity and that "the walls of separation do not reach up to heaven"). There was also the conviction that whatever way and at whatever time the Great Church of the Future comes, it will necessarily include all that is of value from all these traditions, and all their great heroes and heroines will be honoured.

But there was more to come! One had always known of that other people, our elder brothers in faith, the Chosen People of the Old Covenant – so much of their history and their prayer is built into our Christian faith – but one was now making contact with actual, contemporary Judaism, not a Judaism of the past, of B.C., but the living faith of actual people one knew as friends. The breach between us was more painful even than the divisions within Christianity, as St Paul could witness. The unity vision could only be extremely incomplete if it stopped at Christian Unity: all the children of Abraham, "our father in faith" as he is called in the Canon of the Roman Mass, are meant in God's plan to be "one people", part of God's purpose for unity.

And latterly for me the horizon has become wider yet, through contact with the world of Islam and its total devotion to the will of the One God; and through the beginnings of contact with Buddhism, meeting monks who, like us, are in search of union with the One who is All.

So the picture has become increasingly not just one of a fractured Christendom which one longs to see healed, but of a fractured world, though here again there is an awareness of a unity which subsists at an underlying level. God is One, there is only One God, whatever we may call him, and the world he has created is one. The fractured nature of creation itself is all part of the scene – ecological concern and ecumenical concern are facets of the same search for wholeness and for union: that all may be one. And one with that world which is to us invisible – the world of spiritual beings, the angels and archangels who serve before the throne and with that great cloud of witnesses who are the saints; the reality of our communion with them is for me one of the great treasures of our Catholic tradition.

So I cannot see Christian Unity as other than an integral part, a vitally important part, of God's plan for total unity, for the complete and utter oneness of all with the One who is the source and fount and joy of all that is.

If we follow that path we shall find "wholeness", and God will indeed "in all things be glorified" (Rule of St Benedict, chapter 57). If we seek God, if we are engaged in the search, we seek wholeness, for God who is the All is One and we cannot find God in isolation. I am a great admirer of Bunyan's *Pilgrim's Progress*, but as a Catholic I would criticize it, not because he makes fun of Giant Pope, but because he sees Christian's path so much in individualistic terms (unlike that other great classic *Piers Plowman*). The pilgrims are a great multitude, and though we may start from different points we are all together en route.

As Christians we are especially in travail if we are conscious of our divisions, but that is part of a much wider groaning of the whole creation as it waits for the "glorious liberty" (cf. Romans 8:21). The Christ who is for us Way, Truth and Life, is the Cosmic Christ, the Lord of *all* creation, an opening, expanding, barrier-breaking-down, uniting, reconciling Christ, and the vocation of the Christian is to reflect that Christ, to be that Christ, to live that Christ, so that the whole of humankind, the whole creation, can find itself redeemed and made whole. Because oneness is wholeness, it is (how could it be other?) the path to our own personal wholeness. Father Bede Winslow used to talk about *integral* Catholicism – that surely is the goal. But it is a work of grace; our part is to open our hearts and minds, to open ourselves to Christ and his Spirit.

That is the SEARCH!

Acknowledgements

The author and publisher acknowledge with gratitude the use of extracts from the works of other writers, which are generally credited in the main text of this book where details are known. The longer extracts which are, or may be, still in copyright are the following:

"I don't know your name", song, source untraced.

"The Dream of the Rood", in *The Faber Book of Religious Verse*, edited by Helen Gardner.

"The Donkey", in *G. K. Chesterton, Collected Poems*; Methuen

"Easter Night" and "O, Man's capacity", Alice Meynell, in *The Faber Book of Religious Verse*

"Son, I beseech you, don't sleep any more", Michel Quoist, in *Prayers of Life*; Logos Books, Gill & Macmillan; translation copyright, Sheed and Ward

"Up-Hill", Christina Rossetti, in *The Penguin Book of Religious Verse*

"Most glorious Lord of life", Edmund Spenser, in *The Faber Book of Religious Verse*

Fount Paperbacks

Fount is one of the leading paperback publishers of religious books and below are some of its recent titles.

- ☐ THE QUIET HEART George Appleton £2.95
- ☐ PRAYER FOR ALL TIMES Pierre Charles £1.75
- ☐ SEEKING GOD Esther de Waal £1.75
- ☐ THE SCARLET AND THE BLACK
  J. P. Gallagher £1.75
- ☐ TELL MY PEOPLE I LOVE THEM
  Clifford Hill £1.50
- ☐ CONVERSATIONS WITH THE CRUCIFIED
  Reid Isaac £1.50
- ☐ THE LITTLE BOOK OF SYLVANUS
  David Kossoff £1.50
- ☐ DOES GOD EXIST? Hans Küng £5.95
- ☐ GEORGE MACDONALD: AN ANTHOLOGY
  George MacDonald C. S. Lewis (ed.) £1.50
- ☐ WHY I AM STILL A CATHOLIC
  Robert Nowell (ed.) £1.50
- ☐ THE GOSPEL FROM OUTER SPACE
  Robert L. Short £1.50
- ☐ CONTINUALLY AWARE Rita Snowden £1.75
- ☐ TRUE RESURRECTION Harry Williams £1.75
- ☐ WHO WILL DELIVER US? Paul Zahl £1.50

All Fount paperbacks are available at your bookshop or newsagent, or they can also be ordered by post from Fount Paperbacks, Cash Sales Department, G.P.O. Box 29, Douglas, Isle of Man, British Isles. Please send purchase price, plus 15p per book, maximum postage £3. Customers outside the U.K. send purchase price, plus 15p per book. Cheque, postal or money order. No currency.

NAME (Block letters) _____

ADDRESS _____

_____

_____